Peter,

I've seen you in actio
I know you'll keep usi
Soul to stretch for
goal.

your Friend,
Dave Jensen

SELLING
with *Science & Soul*

Increase Your Sales By Applying

The Latest Research on Selling & The Timeless Principles of Spirit

SELLING
with Science & Soul

Increase Your Sales By Applying
The Latest Research on Selling & The Timeless Principles of Spirit

DAVID G. JENSEN

WORLD
BUSINESS
PUBLISHING

Selling with Science & Soul
Increase Your Sales by Applying
The Latest Research on Selling & The Timeless Principles of Spirit
by David G. Jensen

World Business Publishing
3518 Barry Ave.
Los Angeles, CA 90066

Unattributed quotations are by David G. Jensen

Design & Text Composition by Steven Rachwal
Manufactured in the United States of America

Publishers Cataloging-in-Publication Data
Jensen, David.
Selling with Science and Soul: Increase Your Sales by Applying
The Latest Research on Selling & The Timeless Principles of Spirit / David G. Jensen.
p. cm.
Includes bibliographical references.
1. Selling 2. Sales-personnel I. Title

Library of Congress Control Number: 2003105972

ISBN 0-9740577-0-3

This book is dedicated to all those who pursue what is true.

CONTENTS

Section III

How To Use Long-Term Strategies to Keep Your Sales Growing

INTRODUCTION

Another Book on Selling?

Selling can be divided into two parts: the sales process and the salesperson. The process consists of the procedures, tools, and techniques you use to sell. It is what you do. The salesperson is who you are as you apply the process. It is how you do what you do. If you want to dramatically increase sales, you must improve both. *Selling with Science & Soul™* is not just another book on selling, it is the first to combine the latest research on sales (to improve your process) with the universal and timeless principles of the soul (to improve you, the salesperson). It then integrates these seemingly separate parts of selling into a unique system that predictably increases sales. (If you want to see if there's something new for you here, take the short quiz in APPENDIX C.)

Before we dive into how *Selling with Science & Soul™* increases sales, you might find it helpful to hear a little bit about my varied (and somewhat checkered) past. I think you'll see that my practical experience in research, teaching, sales, and management were the seeds for this book. Of course, you may not give two hoots about my background or how this book was born. So feel free to skip this brief section.

Inspired to Write

The graduate program I attended at the University of Wisconsin during the late 1970's had a strong emphasis on research. It even required an internship to fulfill the degree requirements. I was accepted as an intern at University of California-San Diego. Dr. Victor Froelicher, a world-renowned cardiologist and scientist, directed the program. After three months of working as one of his many students, I was delighted when he asked me to stay and work for him. I spent the next five years coordinating, presenting, and publishing (*and loving*) academic research. I didn't understand it back then, but Dr. Froelicher was teaching me that science can help answer one of philosophy's oldest questions: How do we really know what we know? Or from a sales perspective, how do we know what predictably increases sales?

As our research funding started to decrease, I decided it was time to find a more stable source of income. (You can only pay the rent with love for so long.) So when a manager from Medical Data Systems (MDS), a small medical computer manufacturer, offered me a job as an application specialist, I jumped at it. (I had been using computers for our research and taking computer/networking classes at night.) For the next two years, I traveled the U.S. teaching customers how to operate their recently purchased computer systems. I began to understand what made customers happy *after the sale*. I also had the privilege of working with a few extraordinary salespeople, who convinced me that selling should be my next excellent adventure.

I accepted a "sales specialist" position with Siemens Medical Systems when MDS started struggling financially. This unique position required that I assist my sales colleagues in selling our division's new computers. It also mandated that I generate computer/network sales from my own customers in my own territory. What a great way to learn how to sell! I went on sales calls with some of the best salespeople in the company, and then tested their approaches with my own customers. Five years later, I became the top salesperson in our division. That's when one of my best customers made me an offer I couldn't refuse. It was an offer that showed me sales from the other side of the desk and one that led me to write this book.

Dr. Michael Phelps, from University of California-Los Angeles, told me he was building an Institute dedicated to biological imaging (a new method to non-invasively evaluate disease and therapy.) He said he wanted me to be the Chief Administrative Officer of this Institute because of my strong research background and experience in the medical equipment industry. Although I was happy at Siemens, I decided it was time to grow my management skills and took the job. At UCLA, I continued learning about selling, this time as a customer listening to, and buying from, numerous salespeople. The idea for this book was born when Dave, an executive from Siemens, came calling.

Dave asked me to speak at his upcoming national sales meeting. When I asked, why me? he said he wanted me to talk about sales from "both sides of the desk." (That's both sides of my desk, NOT mouth!) I had been the top salesperson when I worked in his division at Siemens, and at the time he called on me at UCLA, I was buying equipment for the Institute. The roots for this book took hold when I agreed to teach Dave's salespeople about selling from both the salesperson's and customer's perspective.

As I put the presentation together, it occurred to me that I couldn't just stand up and give my "learned opinion" about selling based only on my experience. I needed to do what any old researcher would do—a literature review. I decided to find out what science said really increased sales by reviewing the scientific studies published on selling effectiveness.

The presentation to Dave's salespeople went well, and my literature review evolved into an early draft of this book, called *The Science of Selling*. But one morning, as I was doing some creative writing, it dawned on me that my sales presentation, the early draft of this book, and most of the salespeople I listened to as we bought equipment at UCLA, were all missing one thing—soul.

At the time, I wasn't sure what this soul stuff meant or how it related to selling, but I decided to listen to what my intuition was telling me. So I took a deep breath and dove into the topic of soul. I interviewed hundreds of managers about their changing work environment, digested hundreds of articles about the new workforce, and read numerous books on the soul and spirituality. This book is the culmination of my quest to discover what really increases sales in today's dynamic, competitive, global economy. My answer: SCIENCE AND SOUL. My primary goal: To help you increase sales. My secondary goal: To help you touch more lives, like the salespeople who saved my father many years ago.

Inspired to Sell

My father rubbed his sweating hands as he was wheeled into the cold, dark room. His blue eyes darted from one strange machine to another. *Three heart attacks, one bypass surgery and now this,* he cried silently from his wheelchair. *I can't live with this chest pain.*

"The camera will rotate…" the technologist interrupted his sinking thinking. She helped him onto the padded table, and continued explaining the new procedure. She didn't know his swirling mind couldn't grasp medicine's foreign language. She started the machine and walked out.

The sound of the closing door echoed off the lonely walls. The machine closed in. His silent prayer continued.

An hour later the technologist returned, typed a few numbers into the computer, and helped Dad ease back into the wheelchair.

"Dr. Jones will call tomorrow with your test results." She smiled and tried to sound reassuring as she pushed his chair back into the crowded waiting room.

Dr. Jones did call the next day. He said he was surprised by the unusual results; despite all the damage done by three previous heart attacks, the new imaging procedure showed that Dad's heart had enough good muscle for a second bypass operation.

At the other end of the line, Dad gave Mom a rare hug, and told us that he was going back to the hospital to "get his pipes fixed for good." His prayers had been answered.

My father's second bypass surgery was a success. Moreover, everyone at home and the hospital, including his cardiologist, felt that the new imaging procedure the hospital had used gave us three more years with him. But I think they were wrong.

I think a long list of salespeople gave us those extra years. You see the procedure never would have been done if a salesperson had not convinced our cardiologist to buy the new imaging equipment. Of course, the cardiologist wouldn't have had access to this equipment if he had not sold the hospital on investing in the new procedure. Oh yes, we can't forget the corporate executives who persuaded the venture capitalists to finance the development of this cutting-edge technology. And what about all those researchers who needed funding....

You get the point—a long list of successful salespeople helped my father and touched our family back then. Salespeople like you were the ones who gave us three more years with him—years when words unspoken were finally spoken. Years that allowed us to finally develop the open, honest communication I had always longed for. This book is my way of saying thank you and asking you to touch many more families with your sales.

How to Use This Book to Increase Your Sales
Selling with Science & Soul™ is organized into three major sections. The first focuses on why the combination of scientific and soulful selling is needed to increase sales. The second section explains tactics to increase sales success on each sales call. The third presents powerful strategies to keep your sales growing over the long haul.

SECTION I—WHY YOU NEED SCIENCE AND SOUL IN YOUR SELLING
CHAPTER ONE describes what they never taught us in Sales 101—the power of science to predictably increase sales. If you want your sales to go up, you need to apply what thousands of research studies have concluded works. Sounds simple, yet it has taken years to translate all the data into a simple, yet not simplistic, scientific equation revealed in this chapter.

CHAPTER TWO discusses the avalanche of evidence testifying to your customer's search for more soul at work. It also explains why selling is the most honest profession when done with soul. CHAPTER THREE then explains the three principles of soulful selling (*Be Real, Be Present,* and *Be Deep*) and how you can use them to connect with your customers.

SECTION II — HOW TO INCREASE YOUR SALES-CALL EFFECTIVENESS
CHAPTER FOUR explores the pioneering research of Professor Edwin Locke, the father of scientific goal-setting. You learn how to set S.M.A.R.T. sales goals and why, as my research with Professor Locke and Zig Ziglar shows, "just knowing where you're going doesn't get you there." In CHAPTER FIVE, you'll hear why psychologists measure commitment by the steps taken in the face of adversity, and the specific tactics needed to strengthen your commitment to your sales goals.

CHAPTER SIX introduces you to the new belief in town, called self-efficacy, and three sales tools you can use to increase this belief. CHAPTER SEVEN then discusses how to strengthen self-efficacy on each sales call, based on an analysis of 37,750 sales calls.

Despite tons of feedback offered to them before, during, and after sales calls, most salespeople never learn how to use this feedback to increase their success. CHAPTER EIGHT takes care of this perilous omission by showing you how to use the five keys of feedback to stay "motorvated" throughout the day.

SECTION III — LONG-TERM STRATEGIES TO KEEP YOUR SALES GROWING
Section III turns the spotlight on the scientific strategies needed to keep your sales growing over the long haul. CHAPTER NINE discusses why Professor Churchill's analysis of 409 separate sales studies found *Role Clarity* to be the most powerful predictor of long-term sales commitment and success. The chapter explains what *Role Clarity* is and why customers need you to add consulting to your selling.

Traditional relationship selling is dead. Most customers cannot afford to have *a* relationship with *a* salesperson anymore. Instead, many customers now need a business relationship with a team of people. CHAPTER TEN shows you how to add team leadership to your role in selling by using a Systems Thinking Action Team (S.T.A.T.).

Knowledge is not power; applied knowledge is power. CHAPTER ELEVEN teaches you how to practice these techniques by applying the seven steps of *Mastery*. You hear how to get yourself to take the small, consistent steps that, over time, make a BIG difference. You also read why combining old habits with new sales tools helps you create the habits needed to keep your sales growing over the long haul.

CHAPTER TWELVE returns to the topic of feedback, this time with a long-term focus. You learn how to effectively apply systems of feedback to increase sales over the long haul. I'll answer questions like: How do you handle a "less-than-desirable" commission plan? How can you create a consistent method of staying positive no matter what adversity may strike you? How can you lose an order "successfully?"

For most salespeople, calling on top executives is mandatory if they want to reach the top in sales. CHAPTER THIRTEEN explains how to get executives to open their doors, what to do once you're in, and serves as a review of the lessons learned throughout the book. The chapter concludes by presenting a unique model of integrating science and soul.

Section I

*Why You Need
Science and Soul in Your Selling*

CHAPTER 1

How to Use Science to Increase Sales

In God we trust, everyone else must have data

What They Didn't Teach You in Sales 101

After completing my first sales training seminar at Siemens many years ago, I told the instructor how much I enjoyed his two-day class, and then asked him this question: *How do you know if what you teach really increases sales?* He shrugged and said people told him it worked. When I asked if he had studied salespeople before and after they took his class, or if he based what he taught on published sales research, he looked at me as if I were from Mars, answered NO, and bolted for the nearest exit.

I didn't mean to catch him off guard or embarrass him. I was new to the selling profession, and had just left my position as a researcher at the University of California-San Diego. I had spent five years learning that you shouldn't assert something is true unless you can back it up with facts. In short, I learned what philosophers had been discussing since antiquity. (I didn't know that there is an entire discipline of philosophy called Epistemology that explores how we know what we know.) There are many ways to "know" something is true: experience, intuition, experts, science… All have a place, yet only science has the tools and rules to test the truth.

We used to "know" that the world was flat, that we were the center of the universe, and that Adam and Eve were our only ancestors. But then someone used the tools of science to explore our round planet, peer into the expanding cosmos, and look back in time at the fossils of human history. We used to "know" that closing techniques increased sales, that objections during the call were good for the sale, and that selling product benefits worked. But researchers have been gathering the data to say things are NOT what they seem to be.

As I began my sales career, I realized I had been living a sheltered life. I discovered that having evidence to back up what one claims is not common at all. This is true in sales and most professions. What they didn't teach us in Sales 101 is what I learned as a researcher at UCSD — *without data we are all wandering opinions.* What they don't teach us in selling is that without the tools of science to help explore what works, we are stumbling around in the dark caves of ignorance.

Using sales approaches without scientific evidence that demonstrates their effectiveness is like taking prescription drugs that have not been tested or studied. Imagine your doctor giving you a prescription and saying, "We haven't studied this medication, so we can't predict how well it works or what the side-effects will be, but just take it and call us on Monday..." Ridiculous, you say. Who would go to this witchdoctor? Yet salespeople swallow this pill all the time.

Prediction, Proof, and Profit

So, what is science? How does it work, especially as it relates to your sales? Webster's *Ninth New Collegiate Dictionary* defines it as "the state of knowing: a department of systematized knowledge." I like to think of it as a process, a set of tools and rules to help discover what works and why. Just as all sports have specific rules that must be followed to decide who wins, science has defined methods to discover what works. Science helps answer the question, "How do we know what we know?" Following these rules, often referred to as the scientific method, earns the right to claim, "Try this, there's evidence to predict it works."

By the way, you already use the power of prediction every day. In fact, it dominates your life. For example, imagine you're driving down the road, singing your favorite tune. Suddenly, the driver in front of you slams on his brakes! Quick, what do you do? Hit your brakes? Of course, but why? (No, this isn't a trick question.) You step on the brake pedal because you have learned that it decreases your chances of smashing into the car in front of you. In other words, the probability of avoiding the accident is much higher with your foot on the brake than it would be if you decided, let's say, to change your radio station. Congratulations, you just made an accurate prediction based on lots of data from experience (stepping on the brake has worked many times) and science (applying laws of physics helped engineers design those brakes).

Just about everything you do in life is based on a conscious or subconscious assessment of the probability that taking specific action will produce specific results. Whether it's avoiding an accident or using a favorite sales strategy, you do what you do because you believe (i.e., predict) it will give a desired result. Writing for the *Harvard Business Review,* Steveson and Moldoveanu summed up the power of prediction this way:

"Without predictability, people would be too scared not only to take risks but to take any action at all." [2]

So how does this addiction to prediction affect your selling? YOUR SALES SUCCESS IS DIRECTLY RELATED TO THE NUMBER OF ACTIONS YOU TAKE THAT PREDICTABLY INCREASE SALES. Please read that last simple and powerful sentence again. To put it another way, salespeople who consistently reach the top use approaches that accurately predict (consciously or unconsciously) sales success.

Salespeople and sales managers often tell me they know certain sales approaches work because they have been using them for years. To which I reply, FANNNNtastic. Keep doing what works for you (like stepping on your brakes in the car). Experience is a wonderful teacher, *if* you learn from your experiences. (I once worked with a mediocre sales guy who kept bragging about his 20 years of selling. I finally told him that his 20 years of sales consisted of one year, repeated 20 times.) It's always *Groundhog Day* for those who don't learn from experience.

What you do may work for you. However, it's almost impossible to *accurately predict* your sales approach will work for others or in new situations unless you test it scientifically. One of the reasons this is true is because of the so-called "placebo effect," which states that your belief about what will work greatly influences what actually works. One of the major goals of science is to help distinguish the difference between this belief and the effects of an intervention. That's why the gold standard in research is the "double-blinded, randomized, controlled trial," where neither the subjects in the study nor the researchers know who is in the experimental or control group.

"The best way to predict the future is to create it."

—PETER DRUCKER

The bottom line is that science can increase your sales because it has the tools to predict what really works. The more you do what works, the more your sales increase. It's as simple as that. This book is a summary of the latest research on what works (2,000 articles, 250 books, and 2,000 hours of audio-tapes...). It translates all this data into a simple, but not simplistic, scientific equation that predicts sales success. (*FIGURE 1.1*) The equation illustrates that the four fundamental keys to increasing your short and long-term sales are:

1. Having a GOAL to increase sales

2. Increasing your COMMITMENT to that goal

3. Strengthening your BELIEF you can reach the goal

4. Using FEEDBACK to stay on track as you pursue the goal

FIGURE 1.1: *The Science of Selling Equation*

SALES GOAL = COMMITMENT X BELIEF X FEEDBACK

The rest of the book discusses the short- and long-term tools needed to strengthen your sales COMMITMENT, BELIEF, and FEEDBACK. As you adapt these scientific and soulful tools to your unique selling environment, the equation predicts that you will reach your sales goals.

*"Predictions are always dangerous,
especially when they're about the future."*

—YOGI BERRA

The Problems With Science

At a party several years ago, I heard a "well-educated" person declare
that he did not believe in any science because of the holes in the theory
of evolution. I almost fell off my chair (and I wasn't even drinking).
Of course there are holes in the theory of evolution, and in just about
every other scientific theory. Holes don't mean you throw the whole thing
out. Science is all about the tools and rules that increase prediction and
understanding. It's a method to discover what is true. Misunderstandings
occur when people (including scientists, politicians, religious leaders, the
media, and the guy at the party) fail to acknowledge that the process of
science can be as flawed as the people who use it.

Dr. Victor Froelicher, my first mentor in research, taught me to be
skeptical about science, especially when researchers are dogmatic about
their data. So let me invite you to be a skeptic, but avoid becoming a cynic.
In research, reproducibility is king and debate the queen. The scientific
community only sings a song of unity after much repeat testing from
many competing scientists. (That's why they call it re-search.) Believing
that all scientists are infallible is as misguided as thinking religious leaders
are always right.

*"X-rays are a hoax. Radio has no future.
Aircraft flight is impossible."*

—LORD KELVIN, *British physicist who developed
the Kelvin scale of temperature in 1848*

Science says your sales will increase if you apply the well-researched
tools presented in this book because you will have improved the selling
process. Yet earlier I stated that selling can be divided into both the sales

process (i.e., *what* you do) and the salesperson (i.e., *who you are* as you do what you do). Therefore, if you only improve the process, your sales won't increase dramatically because selling doesn't occur in a vacuum. *You* will be applying science in the real world, with changing customers, who have unique needs. If you want extraordinary increases in sales, you need to improve the second aspect of selling—YOU—the salesperson. To become a better sales*person,* become a better person.

"Objects in your mirror are closer than they appear."

CHAPTER 2

Why You Need More Soul In Your Selling

Your Changing Customer Needs a Soul Connection
If you have scanned the best-seller lists during past few years, it's probably no surprise that the fastest-growing segment in nonfiction is the section on spirituality and soul.[1] You can also browse this section in your favorite bookstore. You'll be bombarded with books on near-death experiences, ancient wisdom, and a smorgasbord of *Chicken Soup for the Soul.* These books reflect a fundamental shift at work. Soul issues are affecting the workplace, creating new corporate cultures, and influencing your customers as to how they buy.[2, 3] Consider the following:

→ The president of Dell Computer ($32 billion and the #1 PC distributor worldwide), Kevin Rollins, has launched an initiative called "The Soul of Dell" that is designed to examine the company's culture.[4]

→ Spiritual issues are making the front cover of major publications such as *Harvard Business Review, Readers Digest,* and *Fortune.*[5, 6, 7]

→ New-age thought and old-time religion are booming businesses, according to *Forbes* and *TV Guide.* Religious radio stations have increased 400% over the past 25 years, while TV has experienced that growth in half the time.[8, 9]

→ About 100 new courses on the merging of science and religion spring up every year.[10]

→ The Religious Freedom Restoration Act, passed by Congress in 1997, allows religious expression in the federal workplace without harassment.

→ In his book *How We Believe: The Search for God in an Age of Science,* Occidental College Professor Michael Shermer, who also teaches the Skeptics Lecture Series at the California Institute of Technology, reminds us that humans have a history of clinging to spirituality when living in a sea of uncertainty.[11]

→ The maturing spiritual attitudes of today's 76 million baby boomers are described by Professor of Religion and Society Wade Clark Roof, in his revealing book, *Spiritual Marketplace: Baby Boomers and the Remaking of American Religion.*[12] This University of California-Santa Barbara professor's extensive research reveals:

  ◦ 66% of those born prior to World War II claimed a "strong" religious preference compared to only 40% of the baby boomers

  ◦ 48% of all boomers believe all religions are true and good

  ◦ Baby boomers prefer a fluid approach to spirituality (e.g., all religions have value, and I pick this one...for now). While many boomers are on a spiritual journey, the older generation follows the church doctrine. Boomers are on a quest; their parents drive to church.

→ As boomers make their way up the corporate ladder, issues of the spirit are surfacing at work. Groups such as Marketplace Ministries, Fellowship for Companies Christ International, Chabad Lubavitch, and Legatus (1,300 members, all CEO's) are blossoming all over the corporate landscape.[13]

"Spirituality in the workplace is exploding," summarizes Laura Nash from the Harvard Business School. The seeds are planted. In today's hectic, information-overloaded business environment, your customers are looking for more soul as they earn their daily bread. They have heard all those old sales lines before, and want to work with salespeople who don't use them any more. It's time to drop those lines and connect with your changing customer by selling with soul, not selling your soul.

Ego, Spirit, and Soul

Before you learn how to sell with soul, I need to clarify what the soul is. The definitions and distinctions explained below have been gleaned from years of reading and reflection. I don't claim final authority on this topic; only a few insights that may help you, the sales*person,* grow as you apply the science to your selling.

EGO = The self that is conscious of the individual and most in touch with the external world. Our ego wants to be known and often looks to the outside world for its sense of connection and attachment. In selling, a strong ego is critical. We need one to withstand the numerous blows and no's we take. A healthy ego can drive us toward success. (*I* want to be the one on stage receiving that sales award.) Taken too far, however, an inflated ego becomes an obstacle to our goals. Like a child blowing a giant bubble, we become blinded by our own hot air. An exaggerated sense of self over a long period of time often leads to over-focusing on possessions. Salespeople who become too attached to what they own can lose perspective because they begin to get their sense of self from what they have instead of who they are. (The problem with self-image these days is that it comes from everywhere *but* the self.) Their possessions begin to own them.

Early in my sales career, my ego loved the national sales meetings, especially the awards ceremony. I motivated myself throughout the year by visualizing I was receiving the big prizes in front of my peers. When I shuffled away empty-handed (which happened more than I care to admit), I was depressed for weeks. I finally learned to be less attached to the external awards. I learned to say yes to goals, yes to things money could buy, but no to defining who I was by what I got. I started to use the information, fellowship, and fun of these meetings as internal rewards. I still wanted to become the best, but not at the price of losing my self.

SPIRIT = The vital principle or animating force of all life. Often used to refer to God—a being conceived as the perfect, all-powerful, all-knowing originator and ruler of the universe. Spirit picks us up, lifts us higher, and helps us soar toward the heavens. Spirit is not attached to this world; rather it is our connection to a higher being. In selling, we often hear about Spirit as it refers to someone's enthusiasm, as in "she has the right spirit." (The word *enthusiasm* comes from the Greek *enthousiasmos,* "to be inspired.") Those who get too carried away with it may lose touch with day-to-day reality. They are blinded by their vision. Like the ancient story of Icarus, they fly too close to the sun, the wax on their wings melts, and they crash and burn.

Do you know people who are too "Pollyanna?" They often have a "head in the clouds," everything is always FANNNNtastic, attitude. People who always look at life or sales through rose-colored glasses often have a hard time handling the dark side of sales. It frequently takes them longer to learn how cope with the roller-coaster realities of professional selling. Even Zig Ziglar, who had a legendary career in sales before becoming one of the world's top motivational speakers, suffered from this malady. (www.zigziglar.com) In his wonderful autobiography, he writes that during his early selling years, "I was always overextended financially because I was positive every week would be a great one. Sometimes I miscalculated."[14]

SOUL = The animating and vital principle in each human being. It is the individualized expression of the spirit. Your soul is your unique (i.e., YOUnique) spiritual essence, the real you at your deepest level. Your soul is your exclusive gift. It's the real McCoy without an inflated ego. It's the uplifting spirit that's grounded in reality. Author Sam Keen says that the search for our individual spirit, for God, is ultimately the quest to know ourselves in our heights and depths. That's soul.

To grow the soul is to honor what both ego and spirit bring to the table, without over-emphasizing either one. To sell with soul is to learn how to manage the tension between being too ego-driven and getting carried away by the spirit.

"Ego says, I am the one.
Spirit says, we are all one.
Soul says, I am one with Spirit."

Selling Is the Most Honest Profession

A customer once asked me to install a computer so she could "test drive" the equipment before buying it. My manager and I agreed, knowing I would have to spend a lot of time teaching her to use our specialized software without any guarantee of closing the sale. One evening, after hours of helping her customize the software to fit her way of working, I was blind-sided by her when she said, "I know the only reason you're staying late is that you want to sell us this computer system." My face flushed with anger. I was outraged and insulted that my service-oriented approach to selling could be so misunderstood. I mumbled something about "trying to help," and left after a few minutes. It took me a long time to figure out she was right.

The soul of selling begins with knowing the truth about selling: selling is the most honest profession *if* we are honest about who we are and why we are there. Not *an* honest profession, *the* most honest profession. Think about it, how many other professions are as open about their intentions as selling? As a salesperson, you walk in and everybody knows you are there to sell something, right? (Hey, maybe that's why they call us *sales*people.) What's not so obvious is that most other professions are also in sales, they just don't admit it. When you walk into a doctor's, lawyer's, or auto-mechanic's place of business, they usually don't get paid unless they provide a service to you. They don't stay in business unless they sell you something. Just about everybody is in sales. Yet salespeople are the only ones who are honest about it, *when they sell with soul.*

Ironically, what has given the selling profession its black eye is that most salespeople try to hide the reason they are there. We waltz into a customer's office with fancy titles on our business cards (call me a marketing rep, account manager, business development specialist...

anything BUT a salesperson). We try to disguise our intentions. Salespeople have been conditioned to believe the best way to sell is to pretend they are not selling. WRONG!

In the story above, I was insulted by the customer's comments because I wasn't honest with her or myself. Of course I was there to sell. She knew it, and I should have been open about it. Instead of babbling something about helping when she "insulted" me, I should have responded to her soulfully, "Of course I'm trying to sell you this computer, I'm a *sales*person. And based on what I have learned from working with you the last few days, here's how our system can help you...." Maybe I wouldn't have lost the sale if I had been honest about why I was there.

The roots of deceptive sales practices go back to the traveling show. Stop in town, sell some snake oil, and get out of Dodge. Over time, the traveling showman graduated to the door-to-door salesperson. Knock on the door, get your foot in, talk fast, sell, and get out quick. Those manipulative sales techniques actually worked. Many of these approaches may still work today, for small sales. People still succumb to the high-pressure, 101 sure-fire-ways-to-close-a-sale if the stakes are not high. It bugs them, but sometimes they buy just to get rid of the obnoxious salesperson.

Tom, a top salesperson for a home-security company, recently told me about a saleswoman who applied high-pressure tactics just to get customers to authorize her to send her service people to install the alarm systems. (In the security business, the equipment and installation are practically free. Companies make their profit on the monthly monitoring fee.) People would sign on the dotted line just to get her out of their house. She did very well...for a while. Eventually she had to get out of town. Many of her customers started defaulting on their monthly payments and complaining to Tom's company.

So, those old, deceptive sales approaches work for small sales. But not for long, not if you want repeat business or if you sell products requiring multiple calls or a long sales cycle. Today's dynamic markets and changing customers demand that you sell knowing the truth about sales: it's the most honest profession when you sell with soul.

CHAPTER 3

How to Add More Soul In Your Selling

The Three Principles of Soulful Selling
The three universal principles that will help you sell with soul are: *Be Real, Be Present,* and *Be Deep.* I like to think I selected these three, but really, they picked me. After years of reading so many soul and spirituality books, and interviewing managers about their changing workplace, I was scribbling a few notes when these soul principles just surfaced one day. I do not claim to have *the* truth about growing the soul. I also don't have a lot of data or science in this section (although the rest of the book has plenty.) What I do have are several ideas to help you, the person part of selling, grow as you apply the science of selling.

Adding soul to your selling begins by understanding that *you* need to decide how to apply these principles in your unique sales environment. I'll offer tips, but you need to customize them to your situation. Decide how these insights might increase *your* sales. Do the exercises in the book, adapt and test-drive the ideas in your territory, and then keep what works and throw out the rest.

"The privilege of a lifetime is being who you are."

—JOSEPH CAMPBELL

Principle № 1. BE REAL — Who you are sells more than what you say

The entire sales call was one of precision. I walked out of it with my head spinning. My sales colleague, Mac, had shown his firm grasp of our products, their impact on his customer's business, and handled all objections with efficiency. I was there to learn and provide any technical answers when Mary, our customer, asked. I didn't say much but seemed to connect well with her. A few days later, our boss called me to ask what happened during the call. I gave him a quick summary and asked why he was so interested. He said Mac was about to lose this big order. He told me that Mary had called him and she said we could still win their business if Mac, who had been their salesperson for years, was taken off the account *and I became her primary salesperson.*

This was one of my first sales calls ever. I had no sales technique, didn't know the customer's business well, and had very little to say. When the manager asked a few technical questions, I gave her straightforward answers. A few years later, the manager and her staff told me they no longer wanted to buy from Mac because he was always too stiff and mechanical, and that he never let his hair down. They said they liked me and gave us the order because, although I was an unpolished salesperson, they felt I was real. Mac lost the order because he didn't realize that who we are sells more than what we say. He didn't know how to *Be Real* with a customer.

Contrast Mac's selling style with Rick's, a top insurance salesperson. When I asked him many years ago, "What makes you better than all your competitors who sell similar services?" he smiled, "ME." He went on to explain that he took care of his customers the best. He connected with them and made a difference because of who he was. Rich knew how to *Be Real.* He is now a top insurance executive.

The fundamental unit of the salesperson is the person, the self. It is the YOU in Unique. *Being Real* means bringing your uniqueness to your selling. It means dropping the mask and being who you really are. This first soul principle reminds you, as the Bible says, not to hide your candle under the bed.

Being Real increases sales because today's customers have heard so many manipulative salespeople. You're not still using the either/or close, are you? (Would you like to get together on Tuesday or is Wednesday better?) Your customers have heard all that stuff before. They have been bombarded with hype all their life. More than 3,000 advertising messages assault them every day.[1] Their armor is thick and radar is sensitive. Those old sales approaches now build walls between who you are and who your customers want to see.

Being Real is also important because, in a world filled with facade, pretense, and sizzle, your customers long to see the real thing, your true YOUnique authenticity. As they grow along their own path, they want to deal with salespeople who drop the facade and are authentic human beings. The growth in soul books, as well as my interviews with managers, all reflect the customers' desire to hear from salespeople who are connected to the *person* side of sales*person,* not robots like Mac. As you bring more of you to the sales call, you will stand above your competitors who are probably still selling too much sizzle and not enough steak.

"Contrast is how we see."

Think about today's most popular (not necessarily best) athletes, talk-show hosts, sportscasters, musicians, or celebrities. One characteristic they all tend to have is authenticity. We love to see it because it's so rare. That is what people want these days and why *Be Real* is the first principle of soulful selling.

Real Salespeople At Work

Donna, a sales star in a large medical company for ten years, obtained approval from everyone except the hospital purchasing manager, to move ahead with a purchase. He refused to return her calls or see her when she stopped by. Finally, late one evening she reached him on the phone. That's when he told her he knew everybody in his organization wanted her equipment, but that it was his job to battle for his hospital, to fight for a few more concessions. She showed up in his office the next day uninvited, *with a pair of boxing gloves.* "Let's fight," were the first words out of her mouth. After he got up off the floor from laughing, he said she had won the fight, and the million-dollar sale.

Dale once advised a customer to spend money that had been approved to purchase her (i.e., Dale's) products on equipment for another department, even though she did not sell this other equipment. She told the customer that her analysis of their needs showed that they really needed the other equipment more than what she was selling. They took her advice and bought the other equipment. She got a very big order the following year. She had no competition for the order.

Last year, I listened to Jim tell a receptionist that he was calling to find out what the physician in charge of the medical practice thought about a demo made by Jim's competition. (Jim was going to show his equipment the following day.) The receptionist transferred his call to the physician, and Jim proceeded to ask him how the demo had gone, what he liked, and what he needed to see the next day to help make his decision. When the physician asked him to comment on the competition's machine, Jim told him that he wasn't an expert on their equipment, but he was an expert on his, and at helping physicians improve their practice and business. No dancing around, no manipulative techniques. Jim's authentic sales approach helped him book this order and has kept him on top for 20 years.

Another salesperson I know once chastised a client for his department's low quality. The client later told him that he was the only salesperson who told the truth about their need to improve their service, and that his honesty was a major reason they bought from him.

Michelle walked into a new account to meet with a top executive. The executive started the meeting by barking, "Tell me what you got, I'm busy." Michelle barked back, "I'm busy too. Unless I know what's important to you, I don't know what to talk about. So tell me what is important to you first." The executive smiled and started talking. Michelle was number one that year. She sells with soul.

"Nothing is as invisible as the obvious."

—RICHARD FARSON

Now, you might be thinking, Those are dumb examples. I could never do that stuff. Of course you couldn't, and shouldn't! If you did, it wouldn't be YOU. But what *could* you do? Most of the salespeople I work with are not as creative as Donna, as honest as Dale, straightforward as Jim, or as bold as Michelle. I'm not saying *any* of these approaches would work for you. In fact, I'm saying the opposite. These stories reflect salespeople expressing who *they* really are. They are all top salespeople revealing their authentic selves, daring to drop the mask and *Be Real* with their customers. They were demonstrating their uniqueness, not repeating memorized lines from a sales script.

"To become a better salesperson, become a better person."

How To Be More You

To be yourself you must first know yourself, including your strengths, weaknesses, and uniqueness. In her remarkable book *The Artist's Way*, Julia Cameron describes a powerful technique called Morning Pages.[2] She says that if you really want to discover your deep, creative self, write three pages by hand, non-stop, and fast, in the morning. Anything that comes to mind, write it down, without editing. Don't think, don't hesitate, don't stop. The key is to keep your hand moving no matter what spills out onto the pages. Morning Pages are NOT meant to be prose, poetry, or journaling. You do not need to show them to or share them with *anyone*. You will be amazed at what you learn about yourself, and how these insights can help you sell more authentically.

How do they really work? Julia Cameron contends that these free-flowing thoughts paradoxically silence our inner critic by giving it an outlet. She says these pages help us understand our deeper self, which is very creative by its nature. They give our still, small voice a way to be heard among society's blaring loudspeakers. Think of the Morning Pages as a method of listening to who is really on the inside and what is really going on there. Life is lived, and sales are won, from the inside out.

I call these Morning Pages "AM Pages" because they are the path to discovering who the real self is. My AM Pages have been tremendously helpful to me. They told me to rewrite this book by adding soul to the science of selling. This made no business sense at the time. I had left UCLA, started my speaking and consulting business, and needed to get the book out to increase my revenue. I resisted, yet my AM Pages persisted. Eventually I listened to their wisdom and wrote this book. My AM Pages have helped me cope with tragedy, handle adversity, and celebrate my unique "idiot-syncrasies." The AM Pages have also helped me bring an authenticity to my speaking and sales. John, a sales trainer at Wells Fargo Bank, recently told me he liked the straightforward way I asked for more business after delivering a program for him. (The program went well and I did receive more business.)

Your AM Pages will help you bring the real you to your customer. The nature of your sales will change as soon as you begin to write. My friend Jim, a great salesperson to begin with, had his best sales year ever after he started writing AM Pages. He says, "Understanding who I really am and what's going on inside makes me a better salesperson." Please don't take his word or mine for it. Write your own AM Pages for three weeks, and see for yourself. Buy the book *The Artist's Way* if you want to know more about the pages, or other ways to connect with your creative self.

Use the following incomplete sentences if you want to jumpstart your writing.

→ I am…

→ I really enjoy…

→ Authenticity means…

→ Integrity is…

→ Deep down, I know…

→ I am unique because…

→ Customers like these things about me...

→ I can increase my sales if I...

→ Some creative ideas that I can use on this sale include...

Principle № 2. BE PRESENT—The gift of life is the present

Once upon a time, a salesman made a call to the local Zen master, hoping to sell him a new set of teacups. After inviting the salesman in, the master asked him to participate in the tea ceremony. As the old master prepared the tea, the knowledgeable salesperson discussed the history of the tea ceremony, the variety of fine cups he had to offer, and, of course, the price of tea in China. When the tea was ready, the old master shuffled across the wooden floor, old teapot in hand, and began pouring the steaming tea into the salesman's cup. As the cup became full, the master continued pouring and pouring. The hot tea spilled all over everything, including the shocked salesman. "What are you doing?" he screamed, leaping to his feet. The Zen master looked at him, then at the cup. "You are like this cup, there is no room for me." The salesman wandered back to the office to fill out another lost order form.

Why did the salesperson lose the order? Was he was too full of himself? Too prepared? Too talkative? NO. He lost the order because he was not *with* the Zen master. He was there physically, but he wasn't present with his customer. He was too preoccupied with his knowledge, too focused on his agenda. The master knew it. Your customers can feel it. As another Zen master once said...

"Don't seek the truth, just drop your opinions."

Being fully present on a sales call means being able to leave what is not relevant to the customer at the door. Yet where is a salesperson's attention or internal dialogue during most calls? *What do I say next? How do I handle this objection? My agenda...Blah, Blah, Blah.* Our internal conversation is often everywhere but with the customer. Customers know when we are totally focused on them and when we are full of our own agenda.

I am sensitive to *Being Present,* the second soul principle, because I was terrible at it when I started selling. (In case you've forgotten, *Be Real* is the first principle.) My very first sales call ever was a lot like that tea ceremony. After the call, as a sales colleague and I walked out of the hospital, I asked him how it went. He said fine, but reminded me that during my next call it would be important to let my prospect know that I could BREATHE. I had gone through a 45-minute technical presentation in about 10 minutes, never giving the customer a chance to interact with me. My cup was so full that this customer never bought from me.

I am also sensitive to this because of my view of selling from the other side of the desk. When we were buying equipment at UCLA, I couldn't believe how fixated most salespeople were on their products, their sales lines, or their agenda. They always seemed to be trying to lead us, their customers, somewhere. My administrator colleagues said they felt the same way. The salespersons' cups seemed so full, we didn't feel there was any room for us.

*"Customers don't care how much you know until they know how much you care...
about what they care about."*

Being There Increases Sales

One of the reasons being fully present with your customer increases sales is because it shows that you care about what they care about. Think about the last great conversation you had with a friend: what made it so great? Why did you feel that connection? What did the other person do that helped create the rapport? Let's do a quick exercise: Re-create that conversation in your imagination right now. Drift back. What do you see, hear, and feel? (Please STOP reading for a second and do it. This is an interactive book.) Now, as you look back on this interaction answer a few questions: What did you have in common with this friend? Was he or she paying close attention to you? Did they seem to be "in tune" with you? How did they show they cared about what you cared about?

Salespeople often report that the conversation was special because they felt the other person was *there* for them. And where is there? It's here. It's being fully present with them. It's being here now, as Zen master and former Harvard professor Ram Daas wrote in his book, *Be Here Now*. People show how much they care about us by paying attention to us. Time is the currency of the new millennium. When someone pays close attention to us, we feel honored, valued, and connected because they are spending their precious resource with us. Your customers feel the same way. Undivided attention is the path of connection.

Another reason *Being Present* with customers increases sales is that it helps you to be heard amid the noise and confusion. If you want to be heard, sit down and be with them. The more you focus on being with them and hearing them, and the less you bombard them with hype, the easier it is for them to hear what you say. It is the Zen of hype. Whispering is a wonderful way of grabbing a group's attention. *Being Present* with customers is a great approach to letting them know you are here to care for them. Contrast is how we see and feel.

Being Present with customers also increases sales because you learn so much about what customers truly value. Customers are always communicating below the surface; you can miss what is *not* being said (yet is being communicated) if you are not paying close attention to them. A shift in the chair, a hand to the nose, a sudden eye movement... all missed signs when your cup is too full.

One of the best places to observe the power of *Being Present* is at trade shows. Salespeople often say their goal is to show their latest and greatest merchandise to as many customers as possible. On the contrary, the top salespeople know that the best way to stand out is to be a refuge for customers, especially the ones who are in the buying mode. Rather than overwhelming them with all their new stuff, these pros ask their top customers to take a break from the maddening crowd. The best salespeople then ask their customers questions such as: "How's your meeting going? Which session has been your favorite? How did your presentation go?

What do you think is new and exciting in our industry? What are you going to do differently when you get back to work?"

"A journey begins on common ground."

Eventually, customers will ask the salesperson about new products. That's when these peak performers briefly tell them what *other* customers are saying about their products, and how the latest products relate to *their* meeting. If the customer asks to see a demonstration, top salespeople often reply that the booth is too busy at that time and invite them to set an appointment when they can receive the attention they deserve. Hunger is the best gravy, and scarcity a wonderful sales tool.

This strategy works because it differentiates these top salespeople from their competitors. While the competition yells trying to get attention, the best salespeople whisper. Being with customers is more important than yelling at them. These meetings are analogous to your customers' everyday world. They are so busy, so bombarded with sales pitches, that you will be a welcome relief if you are present with them and not just selling at them.

Another way that *Being Present* with customers increases sales, is the way it reduces the fear of rejection. Think about what fear really is: it's either worrying about the past or projecting negatively into the future. As you become more focused on the power of the present, your fear of rejection decreases. The reason many salespeople fear cold calling is that they anticipate the negative consequences. If I give you a list of prospects guaranteed to buy every time you called, how much fear would you have? None. Why? Because you are not focused on a negative future.

"My life has been filled with terrible misfortune, most of which never happened."

—MICHEL DE MONTAIGNE, *1500's French writer*

A Zen master was training his salespeople on the banks of a river. All of a sudden, a salesperson stood up and said, "A great sales trainer once stood on this side of a river with a brush in his hand, while his student stood on the opposite side with a sheet of paper. And this great trainer wrote his prospect's name on the paper, from across the river. Can you do such miraculous things?"

"No," said the Zen master, "I can only do little miracles. Like when I am thirsty I drink, when I am hungry I eat, when I am insulted I forget, and when I sell I sell."

The Zen master knew that *Being Present* with customers teaches us to focus on the customer in front of us. *Being Present* helps us to forget what happened during the last call and not to worry about what will happen on the next one.

How to Be More Present With Your Customers

"PETERSON HERE," he shouted through the phone. His voice was deep, harsh, and curt. A busy physician with no time for meandering salespeople.

"JENSEN HERE," I yelled back.

"WHAT DO YOU WANT?" he barked.

"I WANNA TALK TO YOU." Did I just yell at a doctor poised to buy half a million dollars of equipment? I'm a dead man.

"Oh Dave, it's good to hear from you. How are you?" The slow, smooth voice sang over the phone.

"Fine, Dr. Peterson. How are you doing?" I responded in my slow, smooth voice.

I saw Dr. Peterson a few years ago at an association meeting He laughed when I reminded him of the story. He said he always barked at salespeople, and that he liked me because I was one of the few who barked back. He said that was one of the reasons he bought from me. We like people who are like us.

There are a number of ways to practice being more present with your customers. The first is illustrated in the Dr. Peterson story and explained below:

1. BE LIKE YOUR CUSTOMER. One of the best ways to be more present with your customers is to be more like your customers. In a field of psychology called neuro-linguistic-programming (NLP), this skill is called duplicating physiology and syntax. I found NLP to be the most valuable sales tool I ever learned to help me *Be Present* with customers.

On your next call, observe your customer's breathing and speaking pace, as well as their posture and gestures. How many breaths are they taking? How fast are they talking? How are they sitting? Moving their hands? Crossing their legs? What are their eye movements? The more you observe and reflect these movements, the more you will *Be Present* with your customers. And the more you're with them, the greater your rapport.

NLP teachers often advocate consciously duplicating or mirroring your customer's communication patterns. Feel free to do that. However, all you really need to do is be keenly aware of their patterns. As you pay more attention to your customer, you will naturally fall into *their* rhythm and style of communication.

Recall the conversation with your friend discussed earlier. What were the similarities between the two of you during that exchange? Was your friend speaking at a radically different pace, tone, volume...from yours? Usually not. We tend to feel connected to, and friendly toward, people who are like us. When someone knocks on our door, our caveman and cavewoman brains are wired to feel safe when the answer to the question, "Who goes there, friend or foe?" is, "Must be a friend, they're a lot like me."

In today's stormy sea of change, your ability to be with customers is a life preserver. Connect with your customers by being more like them using the NLP approach described above. If you want to learn more about it, read Anthony Robbins' book, *Unlimited Power* or purchase his audio-program.[3]

2. SET YOUR INTENTIONS WITH AFFIRMATIONS. Spend a few minutes in the car affirming your desire to be with the customer before walking into your sales calls. Repeat the following (or your own) affirmations:

⇢ I am very relaxed as I focus exclusively on my customer during this call.

⇢ I calmly hear everything my customer is saying and not saying.

⇢ I put my customer at ease because I am.

⇢ I am paying close attention to all the little things on this call.

3. REFLECTIVELY LISTEN. During the call, when your customer says something significant, reflect it back to them, in your words, to confirm you heard them correctly. This forces you to listen carefully.

4. DISCOVER WHAT IS TALKING. You may listen to what your customer is saying, but how often do you really hear what is talking? In other words, do you hear what is beneath the surface of the words? Where are they coming from? Is fear, worry, or doubt "talking?" Or does confidence, certainty, and clarity describe their state of mind? The better you can tune into your customer's broadcasting station, the more "in tune" you are with them. Write yourself a reminder (on the notepad where you write notes during the call) to focus on where your customer is coming from.

5. NOTICE THE DETAILS. Can you accurately describe your customer and their office after a call? What is the color of your customer's shirt, eyes, hair? How does their voice sound? What is on their desk, wall, and chairs? What colors are the carpet, door, and the picture frame on the desk? What sounds did you hear while you were waiting outside? Practice the game of observation to improve your attention.

6. WRITE IN THE THIRD PERSON. Write your AM Pages in the third person for a week. Use your name instead of "I." You will find a distancing of your soulful self from your ego side (which is often caught up in the frenetic pace of the day.) Your soul learns to transcend your ego. In Zen, this practice of watching yourself is called witnessing.

"Witness is the greatest science for an inward revolution."

—OSHO

Principle № 3. BE DEEP—That which is essential is seldom seen
Thomas Moore writes, "depth is the dimension of the soul."[+] He writes
that the soul loves mystery and magic, and that it comes from our depths.
To grow the depths of the soul requires exploring the dark side, nourishing
the inner life, and celebrating the fanciful. In selling, *Being Deep* means
bringing value to customers by being a reservoir of wisdom both during
the sales process and as a salesperson. Thus, *Be Deep* is the third principle
of soulful selling.

Being Deep, as it relates to the sales process, means knowing your
products, your customer's business, and the skills you need to increase
sales success. A major portion of this book is dedicated to improving your
depth of knowledge in this process. The following section, however,
reveals what it means to be a deep sales*person.*

I saw the following exchange while watching public television:

Dr. Wayne Dyer, "What do you get when you squeeze an orange?"

Audience, "Orange juice!"

Dr. Dyer, "But why?"

Audience, silence

Dr. Dyer, "Because that's what is inside!"

Have you seen some salespeople melt when the heat is turned up? They
are the ones who respond poorly when a customer squeezes them, they
collapse under the pressure if a manager pushes too hard, or crack if
strained by their company's bureaucracy. Nothing of substance comes
out when they are challenged because they haven't nourished the depths
of their soul. What comes out when you are under pressure?

A soul with deep roots will keep you anchored when the harsh winds
of adversity blow. (They will, you're in sales.) Growing a sturdy soul
begins by exploring the four C's of *Being Deep.*

> *"Deep roots, rich fruit."*
>
> —REVEREND MICHAEL BECKWITH

The Four C's of Being a Deep Salesperson
In my reading of the world's religions and philosophies, I have found four key ideas that will help you become a deeper salesperson. Adapt them to your way of selling and living, and you'll see that the deeper you choose to go, the higher you and your sales will fly.

№ 1. CHOICE—The immaculate reception
At a local sales meeting several years ago, a sales manager asked each of his salespeople to review their major prospects for the coming year. One by one, they stood up and reviewed their accounts. And one by one, the manager slashed their assumptions, projections, and self-esteem in front of the entire sales team. Most of the salespeople shuffled out of the meeting with their tails between their legs. Several whined about it for a long time. A few of the salespeople made a different choice. Their whole attitude became one of, "I'll show that guy that I know my accounts and that my forecast is accurate." (The best revenge is doing well.) The difference between the whiners' reaction and the winners' response? CHOICE! The bottom line? Those who chose to be motivated by the incident sold a lot more than those who chose to stay insulted.

> *"My first act of free will shall be to believe in free will."*
>
> —WILLIAM JAMES

What kind of choices do you make when you are hit by the hardships of sales? Shakespeare was right, *nothing is good or bad, but thinking makes it so.* The answer to the age-old philosophical question, "If a tree falls in the woods and nobody hears it, does it make a noise?" is...NO! The noise is made when the sound waves strike the eardrums. The immaculate reception is that no matter what happens in the external environment, we can choose how we receive and process it. If this weren't true, everybody would be affected by every situation the same way. Choosing to respond, and not react, to adversity reveals one of the deepest truths in sales and life: *It is in the receiving that meaning is made.*

The idea that we have the power to choose how outside events affect our internal environment has been around for eons and continues to be one of the most profound truths in philosophy. The leading psychologist James Hilman points out that "our soul is what makes the meaning out of experience."[5] *Being Deep* demands that we exercise our free will, our right to choose, because it is the foundation of our humanity. Without it, we're twigs in the river of life, victims of circumstance.

Think of the top salespeople you know. How much time do they spend moaning or groaning about rejection, disappointment, or difficulty? Contrast their approach with a few under-performers you know. What's the difference? How often have you seen the same circumstances affect different people differently? It's not just a matter of attitude; it's a matter of choice. And optimistic, peak-performing salespeople make better choices.

> *"Things don't bother you,*
> *your thoughts about things bother you."*
>
> —REVEREND MICHAEL BECKWITH

Martin Seligman is a Professor of Psychology at the University of Pennsylvania and one of the world's experts on motivation. His research shows that optimistic salespeople outsell their negative colleagues by 21 percent.[6] Optimists maintain an upbeat attitude and positive self-image during tough times by *choosing* to interpret setbacks as:

→ Not their fault — they take personal responsibility without blaming themselves.

→ Temporary obstacle — that which has come to pass has come to pass, so they let it pass.

→ Isolated event — difficult circumstances apply only to this specific customer or situation.

Contrast the optimists' approach with those who are "optimistically challenged" (i.e., pessimists). Professor Seligman's 25 years of research shows that they choose to interpret "negative events" in three ways:

→ *Personally* — it's my fault.

→ *Permanently* — it's always going to be like this.

→ *Pervasively* — it's going to undermine everything else in my life.

You can get a feel for the practical application of this research to sales by multiplying your last year's income by 1.21. Reflect on this 21 percent increase and the three keys of being more optimistic whenever the wind gets knocked out of your "sales." Put this figure where it reminds you that it pays to choose to see negative events in a positive light.

> *"The good Lord gave us control over only one thing,*
> *don't you think it would be the most important thing?*
> *The power to choose our own thoughts."*
>
> —NAPOLEON HILL

When unexpected events hit us, our natural inclination may be to react emotionally. Yet the key to being positive is not to react, but rather to pause and then *choose how to respond.* (Grandma was right, when angry count to 100, when very angry count to 1,000.) Top salespeople understand that if they let negative circumstances or people dictate their actions, they are giving those circumstances or people control over them. Instead of reacting, these peak performers ask if the situation is within their sphere of influence. If it is, they choose to cool down first, then they choose a response. If they can't influence what is affecting them (e.g., the economy, new territory, old products, customers leaving, what others gossip about…), they choose to focus on something else they can control. Peak performers are so busy choosing how they will respond to those things they can influence, they don't have time to bellyache about stuff they can't control.

The laws of physics state that you cannot be in two places at once. If you are moaning and groaning where you have no control, you are NOT spending time where you do have control. It is that simple.

"Between Stimulus and response is a Space called Choice."

—STEVEN COVEY

№ 2. CAUSE—What you see is caused by what you don't
Aristotle taught that to know something is to know its cause. And what causes us to do things in the external world springs from what goes on in our internal environment. Thus, the second "C" of *Being Deep* asks you to look at what is truly causing a particular behavior in yourself or others before leaping to a conclusion or prescription. For example, a brain tumor can cause a headache. But symptoms are not the disease. If a patient died because the physician only treated the headache, the doctor would end up in court. What you, your customers, and others do is on the surface, but the cause is below. Once you begin asking questions about cause, you are on the path to a deeper way of being and selling.

What lies beneath many of the behaviors you see throughout the day? What are the driving influences that cause people to act or buy in specific ways? These are questions philosophers, psychologists, and salespeople have wrestled with for centuries. If you want to be a deep salesperson, you need to tackle them too. One of the fundamental causes of human behavior most relevant to selling is the pursuit of happiness.

"Every decision, big or small, is made on the belief that it will ultimately make us happier." [7]

—DR. SUSAN FRISKE, *President, American Psychological Association*

Aristotle said, "All things we do, we do to increase our happiness." People behave in ways they believe will increase their happiness. Most salespeople know that their job is to discover what customers think will increase their happiness. Yet few have taken the time to reflect on what actually causes happiness. *FIGURE 3.1* is a simple and profound formula that predicts how happy you, your customers, or anyone will be during or after ANYTHING.

FIGURE 3.1

$$HAPPINESS = EXPERIENCE - EXPECTATIONS$$

This formula says that your level of happiness with any event, situation, or sale is equal to how you choose to perceive that experience minus your expectations prior to the event. Let's see how it applies to something you probably do all the time, then how to use it in sales. Think about the last time you were disappointed after seeing a movie or dining out at a restaurant. On a scale of 1 to 10, what score would you assign to the expectation you had *prior to* that experience? (Go ahead, pick a high number if you had high expectations.) Next, on a scale of 1 to 10, what score would you assign to the experience immediately *after* you had the experience? (Pick a low number if you had a lousy experience.) If you do the math (experience – expectations), you have your "happiness score." If expectations were very high (someone told you how great the movie or restaurant would be) and your experience was low (near the end of the movie or dinner you start thinking about what you didn't like), the number is negative. If your subtraction gives you the number zero, the formula says you are satisfied. Whatever number you come up with, it represents how happy or satisfied you feel, overall, after any event or situation.

Think of all the ways this formula plays out, *subconsciously,* every day: The sports team or athlete that is "expected" to win, but falls short. Or the underdog that delights the home crowd by far exceeding expectations by merely reaching the playoffs. How about freeway traffic? You're breezing along at 65 MPH, when all of a sudden, traffic comes to a complete stop. The radio informs you about the accident up ahead. You groan, *Oh no! I am going to be late if we don't start moving.* So, you start praying for *any* movement. And your prayer works! You start moving, slowly at first. How do you feel when you start clicking along at 20, 30, then 40 MPH? Pretty good, right? Why? Because your expectations became so low when you were stuck in the logjam.

Larry, Vice President of Client Services at IMPAC Medical Systems, says the equation helped him understand why some of their long-time customers were complaining about IMPAC's highly rated service. Over the years, these customers had come to expect immediate help from IMPAC's technical support group. The problem was that IMPAC had grown so fast recently that they now had to screen or "triage" all service calls to keep the technical group from getting overwhelmed. This meant that customers were not always getting technical support immediately. Larry believes that the equation predicts that these long-term customers won't be satisfied unless his service group "manages" these customers' high expectations and then delivers a positive experience. He and his team are considering a few ideas that include: educating customers about his company's need to screen calls, offering customers an option to purchase immediate access to technical support, screening calls better to make sure only technical questions go to the technical team, and surveying the most demanding customers about their expectations and experiences.

You get the point. The cause of true customer satisfaction lies in that formula. Have you heard the old maxim, "Under-promise and over-deliver?" That's *FIGURE 3.1* in a different form. The deep salesperson uses this insight to uncover the customer's expectations, manage their expectations, and then deliver a great experience that exceeds them. The really deep salesperson uses this insight to increase his or her happiness all day long, just like a Zen master.

The formula is not new. In fact, it's as old as Zen and religion. Why does a Zen master walk through life happy? Because he has NO (i.e., zero) expectations. He lives in the present moment, in the experience. He chooses to take life as it is, minute by minute, one day at a time, experiencing only the now. *This* is the day the Lord has made. Be glad and rejoice in it. So, while the formula may not be new, how you choose to use it to increase your happiness and sales might be.

Although this philosophy is easy to write about, it's hard to live by.

I still get caught up in the expectation game. Last year a major client cancelled all their training because of slow sales, including the contract they had just signed with me. OUCH! Why was I bummed? Because I was attached to my high expectations: my expectations of making the sale, delivering a great program, and earning more money.

Does the formula mean you need to drop all your expectations and become a Zen monk? No. Positive expectations are the heart of optimism. In fact, when two professors (Robert Rosenthal and Donald Rubin from Harvard University) analyzed and then summarized 345 separate studies on the power of expectancy, they concluded that this so-called *Pygmalion effect* (i.e., you get what you expect) is very predictive of goal achievement.[8] It's important to realize that it is not high expectations that cause unhappiness, *it's your attachment to them.* The key, therefore, is to drop your expectations as your experience begins and be fully available for what's happening during that experience. Empty your cup and fill it with the present moment. (You will, of course, be applying the second principle of soulful selling, *Be Present.*) After the experience, choose to perceive the experience in a positive light. Choose to ask yourself questions that can reframe the experience into something positive. Think optimistically about the experience.

Speaking of optimism, have you ever had an experience that seemed really negative as you were going through it, only to realize later that it was just what you needed? It happens all the time, doesn't it? So, why judge an experience as negative when you are going through it? For all you know, it may turn out to be positive down the road. Some of my best lessons in selling came from lost sales.

In conclusion, I urge you to set high expectations before your sales calls, manager meetings, and throughout your entire day. Then, as you have the experience or look back on it, let your high-flying expectations go like balloons on a windy day. Choose to see what is positive about the experience.

"Anticipation breeds frustration...
if you're attached to expectations."

Ask your AM Pages to help you apply this philosophy to your selling and your life. You will be flooded with applications. Here are a few examples of how top salespeople tell me they are using the formula:

→ My sales call is focused on understanding the customer's expectations.

→ I under-sell, and over-deliver.

→ Although I have a general understanding of what my customers expect, I always double-check these assumptions during every sales call.

→ I'm choosing to see the positive in every experience.

→ I have fewer expectations when I go to our national sales meeting.

→ I'm less frustrated traveling because I make the best use of my delays.

→ Years of sales have taught me not to judge negative customer experiences. I never know what will come out of it.

→ I wake up every morning and think that today is a blank canvas. I let go of yesterday's baggage and try not to worry about tomorrow. THIS is the day the Lord has made. My job is to paint today's canvas the best way I know how.

→ When a current customer asks me to do something, I no longer respond by saying, "No problem." Instead, I tell them I'll do the best I can, but no guarantees. This helps me manage their expectations. When I do come through, they're very happy. If I can't deliver what they wanted, at least they are less disappointed.

Write the revised happiness formula (*FIGURE 3.2*) on a post-it-note, in your appointment book, or digital assistant. Keep it in front of you for the next 40 days. You'll come to a deeper understanding of what causes your and your customers' happiness.

FIGURE 3.2

> LEVEL OF HAPPINESS =
> PERCEIVED EXPERIENCE - ATTACHMENTS TO EXPECTATIONS

№ 3. COMMUNITY—We all spring from the same well
Last year, the top salesperson for Blue Cross of California told me he
sold a policy with extra bells and whistles that a customer didn't really
need. (His company's new commission plan gave incentives to sell these
"extras.") He said he went back a few days later and unsold them. When
I asked why, he said because he believed the law of compensation was
more important than his company's commission plan. I congratulated
him, then told him that over the long haul, the law of compensation and
commission plan are both the same. He did the right thing by helping
his customer and in the end, he helped himself. Did I mention he was
the top salesperson?

The third "C" of *Being Deep* asks you to journey beneath the surface
of separation, and to celebrate an expanded sense of community. Look at
the word community, *common unity*. The Blue Cross salesman understood
this on some deep level. He knew that if he sold bells and whistles to those
who didn't really need them he was doing his customers, and in the long
run himself, a disservice. He knew that the law of compensation is the
same as the law of sowing and reaping. At a deep level he understood that
our deep connections to each other are what makes us a community, and
that any top salesperson who hurts a customer doesn't stay on top for
long because of our connectedness.

Yet society in general, and the media in particular, focus on what
separates us. They write about the differences between sexes, ethnic
diversity, and the variety of religious experience. Division is the order
of the day. Even in religion, people often speak of denominations—that
which divides. Of course we should respect and honor our many differences.
Yet as historian and theologian Huston Smith reminds us, "We must not
let our differences blind us from the unity that binds us."

This appreciation of both our connections and differences is why

Jean, a wonderful human resource manager at Xerox, once told me to forget trying to be colorblind, but to strive to be color neutral. She was black and didn't want people to be blind to it. She wanted them to see it, but not judge her by it. She knew that we don't need to sacrifice our sense of community when we celebrate our individuality.

> *"If you believe in Adam and Eve, we are one*
> *If you believe in the Big Bang, we are one."*

As a salesperson, this third "C" of *Being Deep* means we need to applaud the deeper connections among our customers and co-workers and appreciate their differences. This also means that we cannot give to our customers, teammates, or company without giving to ourselves. The law of compensation demands a balancing of the scales. It is done unto you as you do to others *because* of these deep connections. Paradoxically, serving customers and others becomes a wonderful act of selfishness. What a funny way for the UNIverse (i.e., one song) to work. The more we give, the more we get. We may not always get it right away, we may not see it in the form we expect, but the law of compensation is as real as the law of gravity.

Of course, ignorance of this law is no excuse. Just because someone may not understand, appreciate, or agree with gravity doesn't mean they won't fall down. The law works both ways; you can't harm a customer, co-worker, or the company without hurting yourself.

> Two ocean waves were swelling toward the cliffs. The big wave said to the little wave, "I'm afraid our time has come. Soon it will be all over."
>
> The little wave looked up and said, "You know what your problem is?"
>
> "NO, WHAT?" foamed the big wave.
>
> "You think you're only a wave. I know I'm also the ocean."

Being deeply aware of our larger community reminds us that we are *individuals* living in a *connected* world. The word *individual* comes from the Latin word *individuus,* "indivisible." We don't need to surrender our independence as we celebrate our interdependence. But in a world that focuses on our differences, we must make a concerted effort to define our community in a much larger sense. We are both independent *and* interdependent, the wave and the ocean. We must sell knowing we are both.

> *"All religions, arts, and sciences*
> *are branches of the same tree."*
>
> —ALBERT EINSTEIN

№ 4. CUSTOMERS—How intimate are you with your customers?
If intimacy means to be "profoundly interior," then to be intimate with customers means penetrating the veneer of customer needs—what they say they want—and uncovering their deepest fears and highest aspirations. Thus, the fourth "C" of *Being Deep* is learning as much as possible about your customer's business, competitors, challenges, and *their* customers…

To be profoundly interior with your customers begins with understanding their overall business. When Professors Wilson and Sherrell conducted their analysis of 114 studies on persuasion, they discovered that the number one predictor of persuasion was "perceived level of expertise."[9] In today's environment, that expertise is best demonstrated by understanding your customers' business before you waltz in. The more you know about their business the easier it will be to show them how your products and services can improve their business. You need to find out as much as possible about their strengths, weaknesses, opportunities, and threats. In marketing, this is often called a S.W.O.T. analysis. Most organizations do this on a regular basis, often as part of their strategic plan. Ask your customers for their strategic or business plans, especially if you sell products or services that have long sales cycles.

One of my largest medical sales was to a customer who shared the organization's strategic plan with me. We put together a sales team that showed how we could help these customers reach the strategic goal of increasing the hospital's medical oncology business. We even went a step further. We were able to demonstrate how our products would help them solve some of their customers' (referring oncologists) problems with their patients. Thus, we helped our customer (the hospital) with their customers (oncologists). We earned this sale because we went deep to create a win/win/win (us, our customer, and their customers) scenario.

Meeting your customers' deep needs means more than just asking about what they want, it means knowing their business so well that you can help serve their customers. Here are a few practical tips to help you *Be Deep* with your customers:

1. Uncover information about customers before you call. Begin your Internet search at www.google.com. It's one of the best general search engines. The president of a company once told me they hired me to do his sales training because I was the only vendor who knew their company's mission during the first phone call.

2. Call customers who are on the front lines, those further *down* in an organization, to learn about their business. You earn the right to call on top-level executives only when you understand their business *before you call.* Use this bottom-up approach to discover who's who in the account. Then, ask these "insiders" questions like those listed below before you call at the top:

   → Who are your "best" customers?

   → Why do they buy from you?

   → Have any of your good customers been dissatisfied or left? If so, why?

   → What are your company's business objectives for this year?

   → When can you show me your business or strategic plan?

   → What are some of your biggest challenges?

   → What keeps your customers awake at night?

3. Go to your customer association meetings. Better yet, join the associations your strategic customers belong to. Jeff, a relatively new salesperson for Honeywell, recently told me his sales are finally taking off. He believes one of the reasons is that he is often the only vendor to show up at his customers' local association meetings.

4. Subscribe to the publications your customers read.

5. Go to one of your customer's customers to learn how your products could serve them. When we were working with Xerox, one of my colleagues visited Xerox's best customer in New England. He brought back a wealth of information that helped us *help Xerox help this customer.* When you visit those whom your customer sells to, ask questions about their strategic objectives and major obstacles. Use this information to show each customer how you can help them serve their customers. That's being intimate!

We began this chapter by presenting evidence that customers are looking for more soul at work. We said they have heard those old sales approaches before, and want to work with salespeople who don't use them. There is a reason why the *Chicken Soup for the Soul* series of books have sold over 50 million copies. (www.chickensoup.com) The jury is in. Your customers want more soul in their sales.

However, soulful selling without science is like authenticity without competence. You can be a *Real, Present,* and *Deep* salesperson, but if you don't know what really works during the sales process, your sales won't increase much. You need both soul and science. Yet putting these two together to increase sales has been tough. That's because matters of the spirit, soul, and religion have been at war with science for more than five hundred years.

The War Between Science and Religion

> "Therefore…, invoking the most holy name of our Lord Jesus Christ
> and His most Glorious Mother Mary, We pronounce this Our final
> sentence…: We pronounce, judge, and declare that you Galileo…
> have rendered yourself vehemently suspected by this Holy Office of
> heresy, that is of having believed and held the doctrine (which is false
> and contrary to the Holy and Divine Scriptures) that the sun is the
> center of the world, and that it does not move from east to west, and
> the earth does move…." 1630 A.D.[10]

Since the dawn of time human beings have believed God was an integral
part of everyday life. Our toil with the soil and struggles with nature's
beasts demanded a spiritual approach to all we did. But religion's
exclusive claim on the cosmos began to decline in 1543 when Copernicus
demonstrated that the earth was not the center of the solar system.
Religion took another hit in 1619, when Descartes reported his vision of
the universe as a machine governed by mathematical, not spiritual laws.
In 1630, the Pope tried to hold onto the church's role as the authority on
all matters by declaring Galileo a heretic. But it was too late. The soul
principle, the animating mystery of life, was shoved out of daily life and
banished to the church pews. Science has kept it stranded there ever since.
Dualism, the separation of the spiritual from everyday life, became the
way we worked.

But machines are not geared toward mystery. In the 1920's, quantum
physics raised its head and said, "Wait a minute, life is not a clock, there
is mystery and magic in matter." The pendulum began swinging back.
The battle between science and religion, which had been raging for five
hundred years, is finally quieting down. It is no longer heresy for scientists
to discuss spiritual matters or religious leaders to pontificate about the
value of science. In his October 1996 address to the Pontifical Academy of
Sciences, Pope John Paul II even accepted evolution as a viable theory.[11]
Soul is making a comeback. It is joining science at work. It's time to use
them both to increase your sales.

> *"Science without religion is lame;*
> *religion without science is blind."*
>
> —ALBERT EINSTEIN

The Selling with Science & Soul Equation™

FIGURE 3.3 illustrates one way of integrating science and soul to increase sales. I call it *The Selling with Science & Soul (S3) Equation.*™ It shows the specific sales tools needed to strengthen your COMMITMENT, BELIEF, and FEEDBACK as you strive to reach your sales goals. The first scientific tool influencing each major variable is a sales-call tactic (*Value, Modeling,* and *Motivation*), which tells you how to increase the effectiveness of a sales call. The second tool is the selling strategy (*Role, Mastery, Systems*), teaching what researchers say is needed to grow sales over the long haul. And finally, the third tool is the soul principle (*Real, Present, Deep*), showing *how* to apply the science. The multiplication in the equation illustrates the importance of using all three major variables to reach your sales goals. If any one is zero, the equation predicts you probably won't achieve those goals.

The scientific tactic and strategy under each major variable are the keys to improving your sales *process*—the first part of selling. The third tool under each variable is the soul principle, the key to growing you, the sales*person*—the second part of selling. Now that you know how to sell with soul, the rest of the book shows you how to integrate science and soul to reach your goal.

FIGURE 3.3: The Selling with Science & Soul Equation™

SALES GOAL =	COMMITMENT	X BELIEF	X FEEDBACK
Sales-call tactic	*Value*	*Modeling*	*Motivation*
Selling strategy	*Role*	*Mastery*	*Systems*
Soul principle	*Real*	*Present*	*Deep*

Section II

How to Increase
Your Sales-Call Effectiveness

CHAPTER 4

Knowing Where You're Going

Get S.M.A.R.T — Research from 393 Goal Studies

I became an avid goal setter many years ago when I started listening to motivational masters such as Zig Ziglar, Brian Tracy, and Denis Waitly.... They convinced me that if I wanted to get somewhere, I needed to write down exactly where that was. So I began my adventure as a goal setter, writing lots of sales and personal goals. Over the years I hit many of my targets, but became frustrated whenever I missed the mark (which happened more than I care to admit). I felt guilty when I "failed." I blamed myself for not working hard enough. Maybe I had the wrong goals or visualized them poorly. I thought missing goals meant I must have been doing something wrong in the goal-setting process. It took me years to discover a few facts about the science of goal setting.

The first fact was buried in the extraordinary book, *Goal Setting and Task Performance*.[1] Its perceptive authors, Drs. Edwin A. Locke (Professor of Business and Management at the University of Maryland) and Gary Latham (Professor of Business and Management at the University of Washington), summarize 393 separate research studies on goal setting, involving 40,000 subjects (including salespeople) performing 88 different tasks, in eight different countries, over time spans ranging from minutes to years. According to their research, the *probability* of reaching a goal increases if you:

→ Set specific and difficult goals

→ Limit the number of goals

→ Create short-term and long-term goals

Professors Locke and Latham aren't the only ones to address the science of goal setting. Murray Barrick and two of his colleagues at the University of Iowa studied the effects of goal setting on 91 salespeople in a large wholesale appliance manufacturing business.[2] After analyzing a number of variables, they found that goal setting was one of the best predictors of sales success. Interestingly, salespeople who were identified as extroverts, outgoing and sociable, did *not* perform any better than their quiet sales colleagues did. So much for the back-slapping, joke-telling, sales-star myth.

John Hollenbeck and Charles Williams, from the Graduate School of Business at Michigan State University, studied 88 department store salespeople over a seven-month period. They also found a strong relationship between setting goals and selling success.[3]

So, if goal setting is so powerful and predictive of sales success, why was I missing my goals? The first and most liberating fact I discovered after reading all this research was this: *Being a goal setter does NOT guarantee goal achievement.* For years, I had thought the motivational masters were teaching, "If you write your goals, review them regularly, and work hard...you WILL reach your destination." But the research taught me that knowing where I was going doesn't guarantee that I'll get there, it only increases the probability. Setting goals is a powerful way to increase sales, yet it is only the starting point of the journey.

In selling, this means you need to write goals for the year and objectives for each sales call, and then execute a sales plan to reach these goals. This is the second fact that I discovered about goal setting: *Following a sales system dramatically increases goal achievement.* I had been sold on the importance of goal setting, but didn't have a system of goal achieving. I needed a plan to make my vision a reality. This chapter walks you through the process of setting long-term sales goals and short-term sales-call objectives. The rest of the book describes the plan, using the *Selling with Science and Soul Equation*™ (henceforth referred to as the *S3 Equation*) to help you achieve them. So grab a pencil and let's use science and soul to set your goal.

"*Begin* with the end in mind."
—STEPHEN COVEY

Long-term Sales Success
We start the goal-setting process by asking two fundamental questions: What do you want in life? Why? Answering these big-picture questions often provides the steam behind the engine. You can explore these questions in your AM Pages. Write about the meaning of life, why you're in selling, and who benefits from what you do.

Another way to draw out the answers to these core questions is to perform the "Two-Minute Drill." It's similar to the AM Pages, but you write for only two minutes and do so on specific issues. It's critical to keep your hand moving, just as it is in the AM Pages. Write fast, first thoughts. Don't stop, don't think, and don't read ahead. No matter what splats out on the page, keep writing. You won't share this with anybody, so let your imagination roam. Your intuition knows what you really want and why. Use this exercise to hear its call. Two minutes each, ready, GO!

- → If I die today, my obituary will say...
- → The most important things in life...
- → The reason these are important...
- → My goals in life...
- → My sales serve...
- → When I am on my deathbed...

Did you gain some insight into what moves you and why? (You did the exercise, didn't you?) A strong "why" will overcome almost any obstacle.

The Two-Minute Drill also helps salespeople see the importance of setting goals in a variety of life arenas (spiritual, health, family, community, career, financial…). Since this is a book about increasing sales, I will concentrate in that area. However, please remember to set goals in other areas of life.

*"We move in the direction of the dominant images
we place, or let others place, in our minds."*

How to Set S.M.A.R.T. Sales Goals for the Year
The science and soul of setting a goal requires that you get smart. In this S3 sales approach, S.M.A.R.T. is an acronym for:

SOUL   → *how much of you is in your selling?*

MEASURABLE → *how will you keep track of your progress?*

ATTAINABLE   → *does the goal inspire you to stretch?*

RESPONSIBLE → *who can help you?*

TIMED   → *when will you reach your destination?*

S = SOUL. Nature teaches us that we all have unique gifts to bring to the world. An acorn becomes an oak because that is its nature. Grass pushes through the sidewalk cracks because it's expressing its essence. The soul of a goal says you are here to nurture your nature. Your sales goal needs to allow you to develop your distinct talents. To be a soulful salesperson, you need to spend time every day growing and expressing those qualities in yourself that get you excited about selling. When you write the goal make sure your YOUniqueness pushes its way through.

 I heard an example of having soul in a sales goal when a friend in Michigan recently told me that he loved his new job selling insurance. When I asked why, he said because he gets to do a lot of door-to-door selling. For his 20 years in sales he has always enjoyed that aspect of selling. He feels in control of his destiny because, in his words, "sales is a numbers game." If he wants to earn more money, he knocks on more doors. He also loves the exercise of walking and meeting new people. It's a part of who he is. There's soul in his goal.

I too felt fulfilled when I was selling medical computer systems. I liked to teach (training customers and colleagues), serve (helping healthcare workers and their patients with my products), and learn (attending lots of training sessions and listening to thousands of hours of audio-programs in my car). These are keys to who I am, and I subconsciously made them the basis of my selling style. As a professional speaker, sales trainer, and writer, I now consciously focus on goals that bring my gifts to the world.

You too must shape how you sell around who you are. Intuitively, you already know how to do this and you probably already are to some extent. But let's bring it all to the surface by answering one final, two-minute question: *What do you love most about selling?* Write your answer right now. Come on, it's only two minutes. I'll wait...

Now that you know what gets your juices flowing, how could you do more of it this year? Do you want to: spend more time developing customer relationships, use technology better (to track customers, improve sales presentations, monitor the sales cycle...), increase your understanding about the competition, strategize with high-level executives, improve team selling skills, provide input to engineers regarding new products, do more cold calling (I threw this last one in to see if you're paying attention)? The whole idea of having soul in your goal is to make sure you are spending some of your sales time expressing and growing who you really are.

"Where your pleasure is,
  There is your treasure.
Where your treasure is,
  There is your heart.
Where your heart is,
  There is your happiness."

—ST AUGUSTINE

<u>M</u> = MEASURABLE. Do you know how to track your progress? My friend in Michigan is right, sales is often a numbers game. If you want to increase your income this year, decide how much money you want to earn, then determine how to monitor your progress. Let's start the process by defining how much you want to earn this year. Write a monetary goal in the space below:

I _____ (*your name*) will earn _____

(*your monetary goal*) by _____ (*the date*).

Once you have a monetary goal, you need to figure out how many sales and sales calls it takes to reach that goal. For example, let's say you want to earn $100,000 next year, and have a base salary of $50,000. You therefore need to earn $50,000 in commissions to reach your goal. You then work backward from this commission goal to figure out how many calls per day you need. The math is as follows:

EXAMPLE
Goal = $100,000.00 yearly income

1. *Commissions you need to earn next year* = $50,000 (+ $50,000 base salary)
2. *Average commission earned on each sale* = $2,500
3. *Number of sales you need to achieve your desired commission* = 20 (20 x $2,500 = $50,000)
4. *The percent of your qualified prospects who become customers (i.e., closing ratio)* = 20%
5. *Number of qualified prospects needed to achieve desired income* = 100 (20% x 100 = 20)
6. *Percent of all prospects called who become qualified prospects (i.e., prospect ratio)* = 10%
7. *Number of prospects need to call to find qualified prospects* = 1,000 (10% x 1,000 = 100)
8. *Number of calls needed per day to find 1,000 prospects* = 4/day (4 x 250 days/year = 1,000)

YOUR EXAMPLE — Fill in the blanks with your numbers

1. *Commissions you want to earn next year* = _____
2. *Average commission earned on each sale* = _____
3. *Number sales you need to achieve your desired yearly income* = _____
4. *The percent of your qualified prospects who become customers (closing ratio)* = _____
5. *Number of qualified prospects needed to achieve your desired income* = _____
6. *Percent of all prospects who become qualified prospects (prospect ratio)* = _____
7. *Number of prospects you need to call to find qualified prospects* = _____
8. *Number of calls you need to make per day to find prospects* = _____

Although this may seem a bit basic, it is fundamental to know your numbers. Filling in these blanks illustrates that although selling is a numbers game, you can improve those numbers in many ways. Top salespeople improve their numbers by answering questions such as: How can I increase my income per sale? What could I do to improve my closing or prospect ratio? Where can I find more pre-qualified prospects? Who is doing this well in my company?

<u>A</u> = ATTAINABLE. I received a greeting card a few years ago that read, "Shoot for the moon — if you miss you'll be among the stars!" Sounds nice. Then I thought, *following that advice could also get you lost in space.* Goals should stretch you, but not so far that you feel like you're going to snap.

Do you remember your first national sales meeting? I was so motivated after mine, I flew home without the plane. I was so fired up, that I sat down and wrote my goal: *to be the top salesperson in our division the next year.* Well, I missed my goal that year, and the next, and the next. Dang, if it didn't take four more years to reach the top. My early goals were not attainable.

Many types of sales positions demand years of seasoning before one reaches the top. In his best-selling book, *The Fifth Discipline,* Peter Senge at MIT compares the stretch between where you are and where you want to go to a rubber band.[2] He points out that there is an ongoing tension between Vision (where you want to go) and Reality (the demands of your everyday surroundings). My vision was so far out there that reality had to snap me back during my first few years. Ouch! My goal was not achievable because I didn't consider all the facts of my selling environment (e.g., product knowledge, sales territory, skills needed to call on top executives). You might want to consider how you will manage this "creative tension" as you set your attainable goal.

To ensure there's a dose of reality in your goal, a good rule of thumb is to plan to increase your sales goals by about 20 percent per year. Of course, the reality of your environment depends on many circumstances that may be out of your control (such as sales territories, local or global economy, your company's products and services, customer budgets, and management decisions). That's why the 20 percent figure is only a guideline. If you're one of the many salespeople whose quotas are set by management, that's your reality. Remember, you still get to choose how you go after these preset quotas. That's part of being S.M.A.R.T. about your goals.

<u>R</u> = RESPONSIBLE. The sun is setting on the lone-star salesperson. Salespeople may be responsible for achieving their goals, but these days most salespeople need help from others in their organization. Today's complex market and demanding customers often require salespeople who are independent *and* interdependent. Top salespeople know how to work on their own *and* with others in their organization to meet their goals. Thus, the R in S.M.A.R.T. refers to your internal network which is also "responsible" for your sales success.

Your internal network consists of those individuals in your organization who affect your sales, yet are "behind the scenes." They're not the stars of the show, they are the supportive cast members in your sales chain, like order entry personnel, shipping clerks, account managers, administrative assistants, and factory engineers. Top salespeople rely on a network like this for information about shipping dates, service challenges, upcoming meetings, product problems, and a host of other issues that may affect their customers or sales.

Jerry, an excellent salesperson of expensive cameras, frequently uses his inside network to serve his customer interests and reach his goals. For example, he has a great relationship with the head of order entry. Therefore, his sales always seem to be entered accurately (which for his company, he says, is a miracle). Jerry also plays cards with the inventory manager at the factory. I've heard them joking around at meetings and seen them going off to dinner. Jerry *is* being real as he hangs out with this manager. I don't think he's manipulating the manager. Guess who always seems to have the inside scoop on the low-cost, refurbished cameras? Jerry uses an internal network to help him serve his customers and reach his goals.

Of course, this works both ways. I knew a salesman who treated many of the people responsible for handling orders in-house poorly. Is it any surprise that he spent a lot of time tracking his orders and fielding customer problems and complaints? His face-to-face selling time dropped dramatically. So did his sales. He was fired.

Who are the people in your organization who are also "responsible" for your sales and customers? How can you develop a better relationship with them? Try one-on-one meetings, brief phone calls, occasional lunches or written thank-you notes to stay in touch. The more you show you care about what's important to them, the more they'll care about your goals. *Be Real* as you ask them about:

→ What they like most and least about their job.

→ What bugs them.

→ Their hobbies, family, goals....

→ Thing you could do to make their job easier.

T = TIME. When will you reach your destination? Write the date you will reach your goal. It is not good enough to write that you will accomplish your goal in 6 months. You must put a specific date.

Your Sales-Call Objective

Jon, the top salesperson in an investment firm in Santa Monica, California, told me, "Before I call on prospects or existing customers, I review my notes about their situation, check their stock price, and any news about their business. Next, I write a sales-call objective that defines what I want to achieve during the call. If the call ends with an agreement to continue our dialogue or touch base down the road, I usually consider it *unsuccessful*."

Jon is teaching us that *the successful sales call is one that advances the sale*. He's telling you that it's easier to advance the sale if you define in advance what you're aiming for. If you want to reach your long-term sales goal, you need to write a short-term goal for each call as an objective. If a call doesn't end with an agreement to act to meet that objective, it is not successful. It might be a social call, it might even continue the sale, but it's not really a successful sales call.

To write a pre-call objective, you need to adapt the S.M.A.R.T. goal principles to the sales call. If your product or service has a very short sales cycle (i.e., one call), the objective might be to close the sale. If your product requires multiple calls, you need to write what step must be taken in order to advance the sale. An effective pre-call objective will answer this question: On this call, what action will my customer agree to take that will move them closer to buying from me?

Here are a few examples:

→ My customer will agree to a site visit, so I can show our new equipment.

→ My internal advocate will arrange a meeting with the purchasing manager.

→ My customer will give me a tour of their new facility.

→ This customer will agree to our financing plan.

→ This customer will buy this service today.

Now you're ready to combine your long-term S.M.A.R.T. goal and pre-call objectives into your *Goal Declaration*. Fill in the blanks below and review your *Goal Declaration* before every call. Feel free to adapt it to your selling situation and type it up.

MY GOAL DECLARATION

I _____ (*your name*) will earn _____

(*your monetary goal*) by _____ (*the date*).

As I make my calls and serve my customers during this time,
I will develop and express my unique gifts, my soulfulness, in the following ways:

_____

_____

_____

To accomplish this goal I will make _____ number of calls every day. I know I can accomplish this more easily with the help of others. Listed below are a few of those people with whom I will stay in touch this year, so we can serve our customers together:

_____

_____

_____

I will achieve my goal because I am a dedicated salesperson, helping my customers experience the following benefits:

_____

_____

_____

As I reach my goal, I too will enjoy numerous benefits, including:

_____

_____

_____

I know I will reach my goal because I take daily action toward it.
I write a pre-call objective for each sales call and focus my energy
toward reaching it. I burn my goal into my subconscious by reading
it aloud every morning and before every call. As I review it, I create
the pictures, sounds, and most importantly, the feelings of reaching
my goal.

"Energy directed by a unifying force is close to genius."

Surprising Research Results With Zig Ziglar
With all the great research on goal setting, you might think writing goals
for the year and objectives for each call would guarantee success. However,
it's not that simple. Another fact about goal setting and achieving is this:
*as goals get more difficult, the impact of having written goals on achievement
decreases.* In other words, as you strive toward bigger goals, the predictive
power of just knowing your goals diminishes.[5] Even Professors Locke
and Latham acknowledged this truth when they wrote: "Across the range
of goal setting studies using different tasks, the magnitude of goal effects
on performance decreases as the complexity of the goal increases."[6] The
research is telling us that, as goals get harder, the plan to reach them
becomes increasingly important. It's like having a desire (i.e., goal) to
reach a distant land that is far, far away. Unless you have a map to help
you get there, your chances of reaching this destination are small.

Professor Locke's conclusion is also supported by research Zig Ziglar
and I conducted on 104 people attending one of Zig's seminars, and
published in Zig's book, *Over The Top*.[7] We reported that those individuals
that had written goals and written plans to achieve their goals far out-
performed those who "only" had goals. When Dr. Barry Goldman, a

former student with Professor Locke and now an assistant professor at the University of Arizona, analyzed the data using different statistical tools, he found that goal directedness (i.e., the process of setting and maintaining goals), significantly correlates with positive life outcomes.[8]

Setting challenging sales goals or quotas without having a plan is like setting sail for a buried treasure without the map. If you want to be a top salesperson, you need a destination and a plan to reach it. The rest of this book is about the plan (i.e., a system based on 2,000 scientific articles, 250 books, and 2,000 hours of audio-programs) that increases the probability that you find your treasure.

CHAPTER 5

Should You Be Committed?

Nick At Night

Nick woke up in the hospital. He couldn't move...anything. He couldn't wiggle his toes, his jaw was wired shut, and his body was in a full cast. His wife Carla sat at his side. Her voiced cracked as she reported the doctor's news. He had broken bones in his feet, legs, back, and face. He would be in the hospital for weeks, in a full body cast for six months, and in physical therapy for years. If he was lucky, he might be able to walk and sell again.

Nick had been a rising star at Siemens. He was rookie of the year two years earlier, one of the top salespeople the next year, and his first-quarter numbers looked good for the current year.

But Nick didn't look good at all when I visited him at his new home outside of Seattle, about a month after his hang-gliding accident. He was laid out on the living room couch in a full-body cast — his prison of plaster. His blue eyes were dim and distant. His jaw was no longer wired, but his raspy voice was slow, unsteady. I tried to lift his sagging spirits by talking about the latest tapes and books I was devouring. I told him how his customers were pulling for him and asking about his return.

Nine months later, at our national sales meeting, Nick used a cane to limp up the steps to center stage. He stood beaming under the spotlight, basking in a thunderous, standing ovation. In his third year of selling,

Nick not only broke bones all over his body, he smashed every sales record in an entire industry. He was this year's "Salesperson of the Year." He had turned his living-room prison into an office, adversity into opportunity.

"Stars are seen at night."

—MANUEL LOZANO GARRIDO, *1900's Spanish writer*

The Three Keys to Strengthening Commitment
How do you stay on purpose when adversity challenges you? What can you do to keep motivated? This chapter dives beneath Nick's remarkable achievement to uncover what science says you can do to strengthen your commitment. (FYI, Nick is doing well and runs his own medical service company these days.)

The word *commit* comes from the word Latin *committere*, "to connect." Where there is no commitment there is no connection to the goal. Psychologists actually measure commitment by the steps taken in the face of adversity. Selling is a profession filled with so many obstacles that the true measure of a salesperson is what he or she does when the storm hits. How do you stay connected to your goals when this happens? Let us count the ways.

"Where there's a wall there's a way, IF you are committed."

In their goal-setting book, Professors Locke and Latham identify the numerous factors that affect commitment, many of which are listed in *TABLE 5.1*.[1] Though the list may look overwhelming, we will only consider the few that will help strengthen your commitment to your sales goal. You can see these in the S3 Equation (*FIGURE 5.2*). The first is *Value*, the scientific tactic affecting your commitment to your sales-call objective. We'll focus on *Value* in this chapter. The second key is *Role Clarity*, the long-term sales strategy influencing your connection to your yearly goals. Chapters Nine and Ten will show you why your customers need you to add the roles of a consultant and team leader to your selling.

The third key is *Being Real,* the soul principle that keeps you in touch with who you are as you strengthen your commitment to your goals.

TABLE 5.1: The Many Factors Influencing Commitment

Value

Role Clarity ∘ Rewards

Expectancy ∘ Publicness ∘ Ego

Authority ∘ Competition ∘ Satisfaction

FIGURE 5.2: Three Tools To Increase Sales Commitment

SALES GOAL = COMMITMENT	X	BELIEF	X	FEEDBACK
Sales-call tactic	*Value*	*Modeling*		*Motivation*
Selling strategy	*Role*	*Mastery*		*Systems*
Soul principle	*Real*	*Present*		*Deep*

The Impact of Value In All You Do

Value is first on the list because it reveals the *why* beneath *what* we do. Have you ever seen salespeople who do not *Value* what they do or their goals? They just go through the motions, the daily grind of life. They are the zombies of the sales world, the Willie Lomans (the lost soul in *Death of a Salesman*). It's not always clear who they are until the storm hits. Committed salespeople find a way. Compliant salespeople look for an excuse. One of the biggest mistakes salespeople and sales managers make is confusing commitment and compliance. People who commit give their heart and soul, like Nick. Those who comply put in their time.

Professors Lydon and Zanna, from UCLA, summarize their research by saying that people who see their activities as expressing their core values are much more committed, especially in the face of adversity.[2] They cite a quotation from Professor Kanter, who stated, "A person is committed to the extent he sees it as expressing or fulfilling some fundamental part of himself."

Connecting to Value Before the Sales Call

Socrates was fond of saying that we don't need to be educated as much as we need to be reminded. If you want to stay connected to your sales goals through the ups and downs of a typical sales day, you need to remind yourself constantly *why* your sales goals and call objectives are so valuable. Here are a few exercises to help:

1. Use your AM Pages to refocus at least once a month on the *Value* you create for yourself and others through selling. Complete sentences such as:

   → The statement, *"Nothing moves unless a sale is made,"* is true because...

   → What I enjoy most about selling is...

   → My products and services help customers by...

   → My coworkers and their families benefit from my sales because...

   → Friends I have made at work mean a lot to me because...

   → The money I earn in sales buys...

   → Helping others makes me feel...

   → I love selling because...

   → The equation, *"Production – Sales = SCRAP"* is important because...

2. Review your *Goal Declaration* every morning. Remind yourself why you get up smiling every morning. (As Zig says, "Every day above ground is a great one.")

3. Turn off all distractions a few minutes before arriving at each sales call. Brainstorm, out loud, all the reasons why this sales call is important to you, the customer, and your company.

4. Remind yourself before every call how much money you earn just for making a sales call. Think of your pay as it relates to calls per day, not sales per day. Calculate how much you earn every time you call using the formula examined in the previous chapter.

5. Listen to motivational audio-programs in your car to keep you focused on the importance of your job.

Nick used many of these exercises to reconnect to his goals after his accident. He told me that listening to uplifting audio-programs and reading positive books re-inspired his commitment. Use these exercises to remind yourself of the importance of having yearly sales goals and daily call objectives. It is the big picture and the little steps that keep you on purpose when the storms hit.

CHAPTER 6

How Do You Spell Belief?

"Great things are done when men and mountains meet."

—WILLIAM BLAKE

The second major variable in the S3 Equation is *Belief.* Salespeople often tell me they already know about the magic of believing. To which I reply, "Believe what? Are you supposed to believe in the beauty of your dreams? Yourself? That the sun will come out tomorrow?" It's time to take a look at what science says is the new belief in town, the one dominating cognitive psychology, the one a Xerox executive told me finally helped him understand why his salespeople were not reaching their goals. It is a belief I first stumbled upon many years ago on a mountain...

Take a Hike

Bob, the leader of our high-school camping trip, was right; it gets cold and dark real fast when the sun sets in the Wyoming mountains. After an hour of hiking the steep fire road, my best friend John was a silhouette against the fading sky, one hundred yards ahead of me.

I stopped to catch my breath, then yelled up to him, "It's too dark to reach the top John, we gotta turn around...NOW!!!"

"OK, I'm coming down, you big baby." His sarcasm echoed off the hills as he jogged down the steep trail, slowly at first, then faster and faster and...

"HELP!!! I can't stop!"

John was stampeding toward me, arms flailing, blindly out of control. I glanced down and realized I was standing at the edge of a cliff. If I didn't stop my best friend, the highway 1,000 feet below would.

I charged up the path, aimed my right shoulder at John's belly, and tackled him. (OK, so it was more like a collision. The older I get, the better I was.)

We hit the ground rolling and kept rolling, right off the cliff…onto a narrow, slippery ledge.

TIME OUT. If you were about to slide off a mountain (or wanted to increase sales), which of the following Beliefs do you think would help you the most?

A. SELF-ESTEEM. *Start repeating, "I like myself, I like myself…"*

B. SELF-EXPECTANCY. *Start singing, "The sun will come out tomorrow…"*

C. SELF-PITY. *Start crying, "Why did this happen to me…"*

D. SELF-EFFICACY. *Start affirming, "I can handle this, I've been training for years…"*

This is a story about Belief. The one that helped us off that mountain years ago is the same belief that can increase your sales today. Of course self-esteem is helpful, but you need more than just a good feeling about who you are to get where you want to go. And yes, having a positive attitude is great but attitude does not always equal altitude. What you *do* need is the motivating power of self-efficacy. (Answer D if you're keeping score.)

Self-efficacy is a psychological term that describes "your belief in your ability to take the action needed to reach your goal."[1] It is related to self-confidence, but as professional speaker and author Terry Paulsen says, "We must not confuse confidence with competence." Think of self-efficacy as a combination of both — confidence and competence.

This chapter will give you an understanding of what self-efficacy is and how to use it so your sales climb sky-high. Speaking of climbing, let's finish the story and see why it's an example of how "hiking" self-efficacy helps when you're stuck.

> John and I clung to the slippery, sloping ledge, shivering in the mountain air. We were terrified that we were about to slide off. I glanced up to my left and saw the top of the ridge taunting me, a few feet above my anxious fingertips. I thought about basketball, my ability to touch the rim, and then looked at my best friend....
>
> "Hey, John, I'm going for it."
>
> Before he could object, I leaped up, grabbed the ledge above us, performed the easiest pull-up ever, and scrambled to safety.
>
> Unfortunately, John got caught in the small avalanche I kicked up and started sliding off the ledge. But somehow he was able to leap to the opposite side, away from me, and pull himself up. He disappeared into the mountain's darkness. We were separated and forced to face the night alone.
>
> As John's eyes pierced the darkness, searching for the trail, his thoughts drifted back to childhood lessons he had learned about hiking from his Uncle George. Within minutes, he had a plan of action. Because he was worried about stumbling off the cliff in the pitch-black mountain night, he threw little stones in front of him as he hiked. If he heard them hit solid ground, he took a few steps in that direction. If there was no sound, he figured this was a good sign not to walk that way. John made it safely down the mountain because he believed he could take the action to get where he wanted to go. He had high hiking self-efficacy.
>
> As for me, well, that's a different story. My plan was less effective. Once I was safely perched on top of the ridge, I froze. That's right, I froze. I was scared stiff. Although I knew where the fire road was, my path to safety, I couldn't, wouldn't and didn't move a muscle! Hours later, the rescue team's searchlights finally spotted me shivering on the ledge.

Self-efficacy — The Science of Believing

This true story is also a metaphor about sales self-efficacy — your belief in your ability to take the steps needed to reach your sales goals. Research shows you can dramatically increase the probability of achieving your goal when your self-efficacy is high. *TABLE 6.1* is a long list of behaviors, activities and skills that science has shown to improve following self-efficacy training.[1] Of course, we are interested primarily in sales, yet the Table and story illustrate three important general concepts about self-efficacy.

TABLE 6.1

A MOUNTAIN OF RESEARCH SHOWS SELF-EFFICACY TRAINING IMPROVES:
sales
mood
memory
goal setting
career choice
immune system
athletic performance
academic/training goals
healthy relationships, persistence
parenting, coping with phobias and stress

1. SELF-EFFICACY OVERLAP. Self-efficacy is related to other theories of human performance and belief (e.g., learned optimism, self-esteem, explanatory style, and hardiness...). After reviewing the research on Beliefs, I am convinced that boosting one's self-efficacy is the most direct path to higher sales.

2. SELF-EFFICACY IS TASK SPECIFIC. It is not a global feeling about your overall abilities or self, like self-esteem; it is related to the specific goal you are striving to achieve. For example, several years ago I was backing my new van out of the driveway, when I discovered I had a flat tire. My first thought? Well, I can't print that. But my second thought

was, *How do I change this tire? I don't even know where the jack or spare tire is in this new vehicle.* My self-efficacy in this area was low. A half-hour later, with a little help from a neighbor, I was on my way. Contrast that with what happened when I was cycling yesterday and got a flat. Although my first thoughts were about the same, the second was en*tirely* (just seeing if you're awake) different. I was back on my bike in four minutes because I believed I could take the action to reach my goal. We all have specific mountains we believe we can and can't climb.

3. SELF-EFFICACY IS LEARNED. Our belief about what we can do changes with applied learning. Vacationing in the Vermont woods with Uncle George was the training ground where John increased his hiking self-efficacy. I had no such experience to fall back on when I got stuck on the mountain.

So how do you build your sales self-efficacy? Well, Professor Sujan and his colleagues from Penn State studied 190 salespeople from eight different firms, and found that the salespeople whose self-efficacy rose the most following their sales training (and who increased sales the most), *were in organizations that focused on sales training as a learning process.*[2] The authors explained that this learning orientation, frequently called behavioral orientation, allowed salespeople to enjoy the process of effective selling without being weighed down by the pressure of quotas. The targets to increase sales came later. Even salespeople who had low self-efficacy at the start of the training increased their sales if they learned in this supportive environment. On the other hand, organizations that had a performance orientation, emphasizing the importance of reaching goals and quotas right after the training, tended to de-motivate salespeople and thus their sales failed to increase.

Several years ago, Randy, a sales manager from the medical equipment company Elscint, told me how his sales teams were often beaten up about their numbers at their "motivational" sales meetings. I have news for all managers: *Salespeople know their numbers.* Hammering them (or if you are a salesperson, beating yourself up) about meeting quotas does *not* improve performance.

Contrast Randy's story with Jed's, a regional manager for Wells Fargo

Bank, who did it right when he presented his region's quarterly numbers at a meeting a few weeks ago. Jed recognized his top bank presidents, gave them awards, *as* he showed all the bankers' numbers. He never focused on the "under-performers." When I asked him why he took that approach, he said they knew their numbers and he wanted to concentrate on those *behaviors* that increased sales. The entire two-day meeting was designed to help all the bank executives take the actions needed to reach their goals for the year. That's the essence of sales self-efficacy—building the belief that you can take the action to reach your sales goals.

FIGURE 6.1 shows the three keys to increasing your sales self-efficacy. [3,4] The first key is *Modeling,* the scientific tactic affecting your belief in your ability to achieve your sales-call objective. *Modeling,* in the context of increasing your self-efficacy, is the process of studying those who are achieving the results you want, then adapting their approach to fit your situation. The rest of this chapter shows you how your car and colleagues can help you *Model* sales-call success. The next chapter covers what science, based on an analysis of 37,750 sales calls, says increases the probability that you reach your call objective. (One of my favorite forms of *Modeling* is compiling, analyzing, and then teaching what research reveals works.) The second key to self-efficacy is *Mastery,* the long-term sales strategy affecting your belief that you can reach your yearly sales goals. *Mastery* shows you how to practice your new sales skills over time. The third key is the soul principle of *Be Present*, teaching you how to *Be Present* with your customers as you apply the scientific tools.

FIGURE 6.1: Three Tools To Hike Your Sales Belief

SALES GOAL = COMMITMENT		X BELIEF	X FEEDBACK
Sales-call tactic	*Value*	*Modeling*	*Motivation*
Selling strategy	*Role*	*Mastery*	*Systems*
Soul principle	*Real*	*Present*	*Deep*

Models of Success

"The best learn from the best." That's what I was told by Dr. Victor Froelicher, my first mentor in research and a world-renowned physician-scientist, when I asked him why most of the scientists in a particular area of medicine we were reviewing seemed to be trained at only a few universities. Dr. Froelicher was explaining the power of *Modeling*. If you want to excel in sales, you too must learn from the best. Philosophers, business leaders, and creative geniuses have been applying the power of *Modeling* for centuries.

> Poet and philosopher Ralph Waldo Emerson met with an elite crowd known as the Saturday Club. They met once a month for over 20 years in the Boston area. Members included Longfellow, Hawthorne, Holmes, Whitman...[5]

> In his study of 500 industrial giants, Napoleon Hill reminds us that Henry Ford had his most outstanding achievements when he began associating with Edison, Burroughs, and Firestone.[6]

> Professor Howard Gardner reviewed the lives of creative geniuses such as Freud, Einstein, Picasso, Stravinsky, and Gandhi. He concluded that *Models* of success were instrumental in shaping their lives.[7]

On a more personal note, I remember asking Jack, the top salesperson at my very first national sales meeting, who had helped him the most. He said he listened to a lot of Zig Ziglar audio-programs. That day, Zig and Jack became my first *Models* of sales success.

"Great associations fuel great accomplishments."

These are only a few of the many examples I could mention. Aristotle taught us that children learn by imitation; so do adults. If you want to strengthen your sales self-efficacy, you must apply the power of *Modeling* every day. You need to learn from those who have been where you want go. A place to begin your journey is in your car.

R. U. Driving to Sales Success?

Is your car a Rolling University (R.U.)? It should be. I realized many years ago that I had two choices when I sat in traffic: swear at the guy who had just cut in front of me, or listen to audio-programs. Almost every top salesperson I meet tells me that they invest time and money learning in their car. These peak performers know that learning from the best sales models as they drive to the next call prepares them for that call. Their self-efficacy is higher; they are at their best, because they learn from the best.

When I ask salespeople who are not at the top why they don't make better use of their road time, they say things like:

THE MOTIVATION IS TEMPORARY. So is soap. Motivation, like any healthy habit, requires frequent attention. I know how tempting it is to turn the brain off, and the radio on, after an exhausting sales call. Next time you feel too tired to pop in a tape or CD, tell yourself that you're only going to listen for 10 minutes. Once you get rolling, you may even want to keep on rolling. Even if you only listen for 10 minutes, that small change over time will make a HUGE difference.

I DON'T HAVE TIME. If you are in the car two hours per day (the average, according to the Dartnell Sales Force Compensation Survey), you are on the road about 12 weeks per year. Since you're in the car anyway, my only question is, are you spending or investing time in the car? Savvy salespeople know that expenditures decrease in value over time, while investments go up.

I DON'T HAVE THE MONEY. My friend Tom answered the money objection years ago when I complained about the cost of buying a new audio-program. He asked me if I thought I would get one idea, from one tape, to use one time, to help close one sale? When I answered, "Of course," he asked how much commission I made on one sale. CLOSED.

By the way, I bought a few subliminal audio-programs several years ago, hoping to find an easy way to learn and grow. The promotions sounded good: *Listen to the program and let your subconscious do all the work.* But they didn't work for me. Some people swear by them, yet I think that's the "placebo effect"—the concept that our belief influences our experience. The tools and rules of science are designed to help distinguish our belief *in* something (i.e., subliminal audio-program) from the true effect of that something. I haven't seen any good research demonstrating these audio-programs really work. On the contrary, I have read studies that show when people are randomly assigned to groups (meaning they are unaware of which, if any, subliminal message they are hearing), the programs don't work.[8,9]

Time is life. Care of the soul, and your sale, requires that you invest time wisely. Listen to the great sages of sales in your car. Modeling these experts increases your self-efficacy between calls so that your belief in your success is stronger during the call. As you do, you will be enjoying the journey and making progress toward reaching your destination.

How to Model Sales Stars at Work
In addition to being a sponge in your car, be a continuous learner at work. When I was selling computers and networks, I had my own sales territory *and* I provided technical sales support to several colleagues. This provided me with the extraordinary privilege of making tons of calls with a variety of colleagues and managers. After most calls, I asked my colleagues what went well and what I could do differently next time. I listened and learned a tremendous amount from salespeople at work. You can too, if you practice the other form of *Modeling*—learning from the stars at work.

"*Nothing is as invisible as the obvious.*"
—RICHARD FARSON

Learning from the top salespeople is a simple idea, but seldom practiced. Only a few of my co-workers ever asked me for input, even after I became a top salesperson. The few that did always seemed to be near the top too.

Here are six action ideas to help you consistently *Model* sales stars at your work:

1. Ask for feedback after making calls with managers or colleagues. Remember, just because you ask for advice doesn't mean you have to follow it. Be open and receptive to them, yet don't feel that you have to act on everything you hear. The first "C" of *Being Deep* reminds you that you have the power of choice. Exercise it when someone gives you feedback.

2. Look and listen for excellent sales skills at sales meetings and trade shows. Ask the stars what's working for them, challenges they are having, and competitive strategies they are using. Carry a notepad to jot down new ideas.

3. Use your AM Pages to explore what others are doing well, and how to adapt their approach to increase your sales.

4. Start your own mastermind sales group. Meet once a month and discuss sales books. Learn how each person is applying ideas from these books to their selling.

5. Learn from lousy salespeople. Even poor performers do some things well. (Plus, you learn what not to do.) I once worked with a salesman who only did one thing well; he always looked great. So one day I asked him how he did it, especially after those long, suit-wrinkling hours on the road. That's when I learned to change clothes in the car, and to stop in the restroom to check my appearance before each sales call.

6. Identify three peak performers in your company to call for advice. Write in your calendar the dates when you will call them. When you do, here are six questions to help get the conversation going:

   ➝ What do you consistently do that has the greatest impact on your sales?

→ If you could tell me just one thing I should work on, what would it be?

→ How do you stay motivated when things are not going well?

→ How do you use feedback or rewards to stay on track?

→ What are your favorite sales books or tapes?

→ Is there anything I can help you with?

Salespeople occasionally tell me they are reluctant to call peak performers because they don't want to bother them. Don't worry, stars love shining their light. Besides, not many people ever do call them. Jack, the top salesperson at my first sales meeting, told me that few colleagues ever asked him for help. I found this hard to believe until, four long years later after finally reaching the top, my phone rarely rung either. One salesperson did call though, and called often. Last year she was salesperson of the year—again. She called me recently, wondering why her phone doesn't ring.

Call them coaches, mentors or *Models;* call them anything you want, but if you really want to hike your sales self-efficacy, you need to pick up the phone and call them.

"You can see a lot just by watching."
—YOGI BERRA

Listening to *Models* of success is not enough. The soul of *Modeling* also asks you to plunge beneath the world of words to see what works in practice. Too often people say they are doing one thing, believe they are doing it, and yet are actually doing something else. I learned a lot by asking my colleagues questions, and I learned even more by watching them. In their book, *Self-Directed Behavior,* Professors David Watson and Roland Thorpe from the University of Hawaii warn us that our self-assessment is often inaccurate.[10]

Tips From the Top

TABLE 6.2 is a list of suggestions I received when I asked a group of about 20 top salespeople, *What sales tips have you received from your favorite role model or mentor?* Decide which ones might work for you and then adapt them to your style.

TABLE 6.2: Practical Tips From The Top

> → Keep a separate file on each customer.
> → Don't make phone calls immediately before sales calls.
> → Review notes before each call.
> → Take notes during each call.
> → Ask, don't tell. Telling is not selling.
> → Ask for referrals after every sale.
> → Calculate how much you get paid for every cold call you make.
> → Remind yourself when working late that the competition is sleeping.
> → Make your own rules; don't play by those set by the competition.
> → Never badmouth the competition.
> → Maintain healthy eating, sleeping, and living habits.

EXERCISES

Try the exercises below to anchor the lessons taught in this chapter. The key to building your self-efficacy is taking small steps every day, beginning today. *There is no time except the present.*

1. Peak performers continually build their belief that they can take the actions required to increase sales by *Modeling* in their car. Write the title of at least one book or audio-program you will purchase now. Follow the recommendation of the top salesperson you call.

2. Write the name of at least one of the top salespeople in your company, their phone numbers, and the dates you will call them to ask for advice.

3. Write about your *Beliefs* in your AM Pages this week. Remember, these pages are three pages of fast, brain-dump writing. No stopping, no editing, no judging, and no rereading. Just write flash, first thoughts. Here are a few statements to keep in mind as you write:

   → My Beliefs come from...

   → My sales skills are...

   → Role models in my life...

   → Time in my car...

4. I _____ (*print your name*) hereby commit on this day _____ to spend at least 20 minutes every day, for the next 40 days, Modeling sales skills. These 20 minutes include listening to my Rolling University in the car and Modeling salespeople at work. I know that investing in the sages of sales will help me reach my destination as I enjoy the journey. As I stop, look, and learn from the top salespeople in my company, I am growing my ability to serve my customers and reach my sales goals. I commit to this 40-day trial because I know, NOW is the seed for later.

   _____ (Signature)

CHAPTER 7

Modeling 37,750 Sales Calls

The Science of Purchasing—How Customers Really Buy

In sales, *Modeling* is the process of studying those who have achieved the results you want, then adapting their approach to your selling style and customers. The science of sales-call *Modeling* presented in this chapter teaches you how to build your self-efficacy based on an analysis of 37,750 sales calls. That number is a calculation based on the total number of sales calls reviewed by the research presented, combined with the number of sales calls I have been involved in as a salesperson, sales coach, and buying executive.

To *Model* what works in selling, I begin with what customers think and do when buying. Although none of the sales books I've read reviewed the research on how customers actually buy, I think it's important to base a selling approach on the customers' purchasing process. Science says that if you know how they buy, it increases the chances they will buy from you.

Professor Woodruff and his colleagues at the University of Tennessee have studied consumers' perception of satisfaction and value for years.[1] They point out that when consumers choose to buy or not to buy (THAT is the question in sales), they make a value decision between desirable attributes (i.e., that which is desired in a product) compared to sacrifice attributes (i.e., that which is given up to buy and use a product). They report that consumers make this decision based on a number of "value dimensions," including:

1. **VALUE TRIGGERS.** These are events that begin changing the consumers' perception of their situation. For example, if a health club moved into the neighborhood it might stimulate thoughts about losing weight or getting in shape. Or seeing new clothes as you walk down the street could provoke notions about those old, worn-out shoes you're still wearing. A trigger event brings to the surface an awareness that a consumer's present circumstances might change.

2. **DEVALUATION OF WHAT THEY HAVE.** Consumers then begin accentuating the negative aspects of their current situation. In their review article, Professor Woodruff and his co-authors cite the example of a woman who bought a new pair of shoes. She told researchers that her favorite old shoes were starting to look shabby. She focused on all the places where they were wearing out. She was also worried that they didn't look good with a new dress. In this stage of the purchasing process, she was beginning to feel the impact of her concerns about her shoes. Subconsciously, she was creating the discomfort that would motivate her to enter the next stage.

3. **VALUE-IN-USE.** This occurs as consumers start imagining the benefits of using the new product. If someone is considering buying a health-club membership, they don't think much about the fancy features of the equipment, they imagine how they are going to feel using the equipment. When someone thinks about buying a sports utility vehicle (SUV), at this stage of the purchasing process they begin picturing how they will enjoy using the extra space. If the woman in the previous example had associated discomfort with her old shoes, this is when she would start getting excited about the benefits of owning the new shoes. People don't buy features, they buy the benefits those features provide.

4. **POSSESSION VALUE.** This refers to the anticipated pleasure people imagine they will feel when they own a product. Think of it as the payoff, at the emotional level, consumers envision they will feel when they posses the product. The person about to buy that health-club

membership starts feeling the joy of losing weight. A father might imagine the good feelings associated with being able to transport half the soccer team in his new SUV. The woman buying new shoes would start anticipating the responses she'd receive from her friends or spouse, such as how they match her red dress.

These value dimensions shed light on what customers are thinking when they buy, but they don't tell us exactly how they buy. To use the valuable research described above on a sales call, we need to examine the process customers go through when they actually make purchasing decisions. Professor Michele Bunn, from State University of New York, surveyed 826 purchasing managers from 52 different industries to address this very issue. He found that managers followed four discrete activities when making buying decisions.[2] His research on purchasing patterns, combined with what we now know about value dimensions, provide a very powerful platform for sales-call success. Let's first quickly describe the four activities Professor Bunn says most managers engage in when they buy, then apply all the research to your sales calls. The four activities are:

1. SEARCH FOR INFORMATION. Complex buying decisions involve tons of data. Managers need to consider such issues as: how much they need to learn about their situation and the products, who the vendors might be, what their organization's negotiating strength is, and so on.

2. APPLY PROCEDURAL CONTROL. Policies, procedures, and precedent operate as guides for most purchasing decisions. These constitute the norms or the accepted "way we buy things around here." If the purchases are routine, managers often follow their own simple approach, often unconsciously. However, the more complex the purchase or bureaucratic the organization, the more organized and elaborate these procedures tend to be.

3. USE ANALYSIS TECHNIQUES. Managers also need to make sense of the information involved in many decisions. They must evaluate

their options and bring structure to the process using various techniques. The tools used to analyze a purchasing decision might include financial models that apply return on investment (ROI) calculations or risk assessments that attempt to predict the impact of various purchase options. How sophisticated the analysis is and which one managers use depends on the complexity and nature of the purchase. When I was with Siemens, I often employed financial approaches, called "pro forma" analysis, as an aid as customers analyzed their situation. I used it to help them make sense (and cents) of the numerous variables that needed to be considered as they evaluated the impact of their potential purchase.

4. FOCUS PROACTIVELY. The impact of an important purchase on the organization's strategy must be considered. Being proactively focused means considering how a purchasing decision affects an organization's strategic objectives and long-range needs. This is why you should try to obtain your customer's strategic or business plan (if your products or services affect it).

Now, let's put all this research into a practical framework you can use for every sales call. We begin by dividing the sales call into four distinct stages or phases:

    I. PLAN — *develop a pre-call ritual*

    II. OPEN — *answer friend or foe*

    III. DIAGNOSE — *ask P.A.I.D. questions*

    IV. PRESCRIBE — *earn agreement to take the next step*

What To Do During The Four Phases of Every Sales Call
I. PLAN — *develop a pre-call ritual*
Webster's Dictionary defines ritual as "any formal and customarily repeated act or series of acts." Most rituals are designed to concentrate our attention on something of importance and put us in the desired

frame of mind. Rituals have been observed in religion and adapted by peak performers in many professions for eons. Watch top athletes before a big game, or sneak a peek at the best lawyers, doctors, entertainers, executives, speakers, and salespeople, and you'll see them faithfully following a detailed sequence of procedures prior to their performance. Peak performers employ rituals to rivet their attention on their intention. Science says that if you want to put your customers in a positive and buying mood, put rituals to work for you.

"A sale well begun is half done."

Professor Herbert Bless from the University of Mannheim in Germany and his colleagues studied 257 college students to determine the effect of mood on attitude and persuasiveness.[3] Subjects were first put in either a good mood (by asking them to write a vivid account of a very happy event in their life, or bad mood (by asking them to write a vivid account of a very sad event). Then researchers assigned the students to listen to a recorded message containing either a strong or a weak argument about the increase in their student service fees. Those who were in the "good mood group" were convinced by both the strong and weak arguments and were less fussy about the details of either argument. Those in the "bad mood group" were not convinced by the weak argument and were fussy about the details of both arguments. This study reminds us of something we all know intuitively: *we can influence our customers' receptivity to our message (i.e., our arguments) if we make sure they are in a good mood.* And what better way to put them in a positive mind-set than by first making sure we have focused our own attitude with a pre-call ritual? Feel free to adapt the steps outlined below to fit your unique selling style as you create your own ritual, because science says that a happy customer is a buying customer.

1. THE CALL BEGINS BEFORE YOU CALL. The more you know about your customer value triggers, purchasing policies, and long-term strategies before you call, the more successful the call. In fact, gathering information about your customer's present circumstances

prior to the sales call earns you the right to make the call. So before you pick up a phone or drive to see a customer, do a little homework by answering questions such as: *What's going on in their world today? Whom can I call to learn about recent changes or triggering events? Is there an inside coach or advocate from whom I can get the inside scoop? What's their stock price and trend? How could I use the Internet to gather information about their business situation and challenges? What's happening to my customer's customer?*

2. ARRIVE ABOUT TEN MINUTES BEFORE YOUR APPOINTMENT. Sit quietly in your car, thinking about what you will accomplish on this sales call. Use all your senses to create a rich, 3-D representation of the call. Imagine the pictures, sounds and feelings you'll have as you interact with your customer. Place yourself in the picture as if you're experiencing this successful call in real time. (1 min.)

3. REVIEW ANY WRITTEN NOTES ABOUT THIS CUSTOMER FROM PREVIOUS SALES CALLS. (I strongly encourage you to take notes during your calls.) Look for clues about the customer's wants, needs, desires, goals, fears, and pain. What are their "hot buttons?" (2 min.)

4. BEGIN A BRIEF BRAINSTORMING EXERCISE. Take out a blank sheet of paper and write very short answers to questions like: *Who are the key players? What are their major challenges? What do they highly value? How can I serve this customer on this call? How will helping them with their problems advance the sale? What should the next step be? What do I need to learn on this call to earn their agreement to take the next step with me?* (2 min.)

5. WRITE A SHORT, ONE-SENTENCE OBJECTIVE FOR THIS CALL. Apply the S.M.A.R.T. (i.e., *Soulful, Measurable, Attainable, Responsible,* and *Timed*) goal principles you learned earlier. If your products or services have a very short sales cycle (i.e., one call), the objective might be to close the sale. If your product requires multiple calls, write exactly what the next step should be in order to advance the sale. Remember Jon's lesson? You can only advance the sale if you

know, in advance, what you're aiming for. This pre-call objective is your bulls-eye. It should answer this question: What action will my customer agree to take on this call that will move them closer to buying from me? (2 min.)

6. FOLLOWING YOUR PRE-CALL OBJECTIVE, LIST A FEW QUESTIONS THAT WILL HELP YOU EARN AGREEMENT TO TAKE THE NEXT STEP. The diagnosis section of this chapter, Phase III of the sales call, discusses these questions in detail. (2 min.)

7. FINALLY, STEP OUT OF YOUR CAR AND STRIDE BOLDLY TO YOUR CUSTOMER'S OFFICE. Park far away to give yourself time to positively affirm your intention as you head for their entrance. March confidently in the direction of your dreams, shoulders back, head up, smile on your face. Stop in the restroom before seeing your customer. Perform a quick checkup to make sure what you see in the mirror matches what you feel inside. Go forth and open the call.

II. OPEN — *answer friend or foe*

Imagine you and the clan are hanging out in the cave one evening, warming your hands around the fire, about 20,000 years ago. Suddenly, you hear twigs cracking under heavy steps outside the cave. The sound gets louder as the intruder gets closer and closer. Your heart starts racing, muscles tighten, and your eyes strain to pierce the outside darkness. Survival instincts kick in, you grab your spear, and your reptilian brain screams, "Who goes there, friend or foe?"

Scientists tell us that our reptilian brains (yes, we still have them) have been asking this question ever since. The key to a great opening is getting your customer's brain to answer "friend." Therefore, your early sales-call behavior, especially with new prospects or customer you don't know well, makes a big impression. According to Professors Ambad and Rosenthal, first impressions are fast and last.[*] These scientists summarized 44 separate studies on first impressions, and concluded that people make accurate and lasting judgments in less than one-half second. Although they didn't specifically discuss sales, their research suggests that a well-developed opening is critical. Here are a few guidelines to ensure that your customer subconsciously answers "friend" when you come knocking:

1. DO NOT CHIT CHAT. You want to come across as friendly, yet not as someone pretending to be a friend if you are not. If you don't know your customer well, don't ask about their kids, hobbies or what they did last weekend. Time is the currency of the new millennium, and most customers are busy professionals. Of course, there are exceptions to this rule. Lingering over a few pleasantries is expected in Japan and some parts of the United States. (Last week I saw an old business acquaintance at a meeting in Atlanta. Although we hadn't spoken in a year, most of her warm, friendly questions centered on my personal life.) If you know your customer well, ask about Aunt Martha's surgery. But the general rule during the opening is that less is more. The soul principle of *Be Real* also applies as you make your first impression.

2. DO NOT TALK ABOUT BENEFITS. Talking about your product or its benefits early in the sales call increases the risk of objections. Even if your customer indicated that something was beneficial last call, don't assume it is still important. A lot of water may have gone under the bridge since last you called. Opening with benefit statements also allows the customer to start asking you questions, thereby taking early control of the conversation.

3. DO NOT OVER-FOCUS ON PERSONALITY STYLE. Have you learned about personality styles (e.g., Myers-Briggs and DISC)? The key idea behind these theories, as they relate to sales anyway, is that your customers have different styles of communication and you should approach each of them according to *their* style, not yours. It makes sense, too. You don't want to approach a hard-driving control freak with a touchy-feely sales presentation. I loved learning that stuff, and know a lot of salespeople who find it helpful. However, I had a hard time using it on sales calls. Sometimes I found myself

so preoccupied with analyzing the customer personality, I would forget to *Be Real, Present,* or *Deep* with them. Over-analysis caused my paralysis. (What worked best for me was applying the NLP skills discussed in Chapter Three.) Customers will think "friend" when you come knocking if you are like them. So, if you find it helpful to analyze their style, then adapt yours to fit theirs, great. But don't get so caught up in it that you forget to *Be Real, Present,* and *Deep.*

4. DO ASK ABOUT THEIR PRESENT CIRCUMSTANCES. As discussed earlier, as part of your pre-call ritual, it is important to write a few questions to ask during the call. At least one of those questions needs to be about their current situation. This question serves as the bridge to the diagnostic stage of the sales call.

"Prescription without diagnosis is malpractice."

III. DIAGNOSE — *ask P.A.I.D. questions*

The buying process is a moving experience. The research presented earlier indicates that customers buy when their awareness of a concern (based on information about their circumstances and/or a value trigger) becomes a definite need (based on their desire for gain and/or need to relieve pain). Your job during the diagnostic phase of the sales call is to first focus on the customer's pain - where it hurts and how much the hurt costs. Then, near the end of this phase, your task becomes to concentrate on gain — where you can help and how much better they'll feel if they work with you. Think of the sales call as a process of leading customers from one end of a scale that starts with *I might have a concern,* to the other end, *I want you to help me.* The intensity of their pain and desire for gain determines how far and fast they move. Thus, the diagnostic phase of a call is about moving customers from pain to gain. When the contrast between these two is felt, they buy. The best way to move your customers through this process is to ask P.A.I.D. questions:

<u>P</u> = PRESENT CIRCUMSTANCES
<u>A</u> = AREA OF CONCERN
<u>I</u> = IMPACT OF CONCERNS
<u>D</u> = DETERMINE BENEFITS

<u>P</u>RESENT <u>C</u>IRCUMSTANCE <u>Q</u>UESTIONS

At the end of your brief opening, ask a few questions to uncover what is happening with the customer at that time. These Present circumstance questions need to show them that you understand their business and are there to talk about what's important to them. Here are three keys to help:

1. Uncover as much about your customer's circumstances as possible *before you make the call.* Use the Internet, ask service and sales colleagues what they know, phone or e-mail other customers at this account with whom you have a relationship, and review your notes from previous calls. Do your homework before you call.

2. Don't spend too much time asking Present circumstance questions because it gives customers the impression that you don't understand their business. Asking a few focused, well-researched questions says that you know their business and appreciate their procedures.

3. Make a list of features and benefits for your products if you don't already have one. Then highlight those you feel are most unique to this customer's circumstances.

4. Finally, before you make the sales call, write a few Present circumstance questions in those areas where you have a competitive advantage. Begin your diagnosis by asking open-ended questions where you can deliver the most value.

→ Here are a few examples of Present circumstance questions you might ask if you were selling computer networks:

- How would your people rate the performance of your backup utility programs?
- What are the major reasons your Information Technology (IT) Department wants to upgrade the system now?
- How do you analyze your data trends now?

→ When I sell my sales training programs, I often ask:

- What questions do your salespeople ask that help customers feel pain?
- How do your salespeople feel about calling on top executives?
- Why do you think past sales training has not increased your sales?

→ Other Present circumstance questions include:

- What brings you into our bank today?
- Do you mind telling me what you're looking for in a new car?
- How have you made these types of purchases in the past?

Area of Concern Questions

While circumstances often stimulate a customer's interest in buying, it is their concern about these circumstances that begins the real process of buying. This occurs when the customer starts thinking, often unconsciously, about the possible problems or concerns related to their circumstances. For example, when a friend recently purchased a new MFD (a Multi-Function Device is a color printer, photocopier, fax, and scanner, all-in-one machine.), she told me she was concerned about wasting time running to Kinko's every time she needed color copies. Think about a major item you purchased in the past year; didn't you have a few concerns that made you start thinking that you should at least consider buying?

Your job at this stage of the diagnostic phase is to ask questions that will increase your understanding of the customer's concerns. It's as if you're strolling down a dark path with your customer and you have the flashlight. Your Area of concern questions shine the light on the obstacles in the way and ask the customer to tell you if it is a real concern. Here are a few guidelines to follow as you create these questions:

1. Direct your questions toward areas where your products offer the greatest competitive advantage. If you've done your pre-call home-work and asked a few targeted Present circumstance questions, your Area of concern questions should hone in on those target areas.

2. Explore areas those target areas fully. Act as if you're a doctor asking questions to find out what their biggest concerns are.

3. Spend most of your time asking Area of concern questions that highlight these most painful areas.

Examples of Area of concern questions:

→ COMPUTER NETWORKS

- Are you concerned about addressing system backup issues this year?
- What network performance issues are you looking to improve the most?
- Is paying overtime to analyze trends a problem?

→ SALES TRAINING

- Are you concerned that your salespeople don't focus on pain before offering relief?
- Who else is worried that the sales force is not calling on top executives?
- Can you tell me how customer complaints about too many salespeople calling on them is affecting morale?

→ OTHERS

- Are you worried about the high interest you're paying on your credit-card debt?
- You mentioned safety a minute ago, what's important to you in this area?
- Are you concerned this issue could affect your strategic goals?

IMPACT QUESTIONS

My early sales training taught me to respond with a benefit statement whenever the customer expressed a concern. For example, if a customer indicated that computer speed was important, I would reply, "Of course CPU clock-speed is critical, which is why we have the new XYZ chip in this computer. It is so fast, it can process a gazillion instructions per second…" If you sell real estate and a prospect indicates that local school quality is important, you may have learned to say, "Yes, quality schools are very important these days, which is why this house is perfect for you. The school system in this community is rated in the top 10 percent in the state."

The logic behind this approach can't be faulted—the prospect says they are concerned about an issue, and you respond by indicating how you can help. But that's the problem, it's *too* logical. People do not buy on logic. They buy on emotion and justify with logic. Just because someone has a concern or need doesn't mean they are motivated to address it. Customers don't buy because they are concerned, they buy because they feel the impact of their concerns. That's because most problems by themselves are not painful enough to move prospects to action. It is only when customers feel the negative consequences (i.e., pain) of their problems that they emotionally buy your recommendations. Please read that last sentence again, *it is one of the most important statements in this book.*

In smaller sales, like shoes, research tells us that customers begin feeling the impact by devaluing what they currently own. In larger sales, managers often use analysis techniques to understand the implication of a purchasing decision.

A salesperson once told me that dentists bought his machine because it improved cash flow and decreased patient pain. Whenever the dentists expressed concerns in these areas, he told them how the equipment could help. After learning to ask Impact questions, he discovered that these busy dentists became very responsive if, instead of jumping in with benefit statements when they said money was an issue, he asked why money was an issue. The dentists would start lamenting about the need to remodel their home for an ailing parent, pay for their children's education, spend less time at the office, and more time with the family…When asked why patient comfort was a concern, the dentists would go on and on about screaming kids, unhappy parents, or the stress of their job…It wasn't their concern about money or painful office visits that emotionally motivated the dentists; it was the impact of their concerns.

Impact questions get to the "root" of why customers seriously consider buying. Advertisers know this. It's why they often show people in pain at the start of the commercial and experiencing pain relief via their product at the end of a commercial. Nothing will create a desire for pain relief (i.e., your product) faster than asking questions that help you and your customers understand the ramifications of their concerns. As I recently told Bob, a Senior Regional Wholesaler for Principal Financial Group, "You can lead a horse to water, but you can't make him drink. HOWEVER, you can get him real thirsty." When salespeople ask me what one thing they could do to increase their sales-call success the most, I answer, "Get your customers real thirsty by asking Impact questions!"

Examples of Impact questions:

→ COMPUTER NETWORKS
  - How did the latest backup failure affect you?
  - If you don't address the system backup issues, what might happen?
  - What was the cost of re-configuring your network after the last virus?
  - How did this impact your team's other projects?

→ SALES TRAINING
  - What's the cost of not reaching top executives?
  - What happens when your customer is confused about which team member to call?
  - What are the implications of your salespeople not asking Impact questions?

→ OTHERS

- And how do you feel about delaying the start of your child's college fund?
- How might the other parents feel about that car's safety record?
- What might that affect down the road?

Do you see how these questions focus on understanding customer discomfort? Impact questions are "get-in-touch-with-pain" questions. Like a magnifying glass on dry leaves, Impact questions concentrate your customer's attention on feeling the heat of their problems. As you stroll along the path with your customer, Area of concern questions highlight their problems while Impact questions help you and the customer understand how these concerns are really hurting.

During a recent sales training program for Wells Fargo, several bank presidents came up with the following "generic" Impact questions:

→ Have you found that leads to…?

→ What effect might that have on…?

→ How frequently has that caused…?

→ What does that create…?

DETERMINE BENEFIT QUESTIONS

Up to this point your questions have focused on the customer's concerns and the impact of these concerns. This means you've been talking mostly about pain. Yet if you dwell in the dark too long, your customer will feel too much discomfort. Therefore, science says your next few questions must help them understand how they will benefit from taking action with you. This is where you help them feel the " value-in-use" and "possession value" discussed earlier in this chapter (as part of the science of purchasing—how customers really buy section). This is also when, if possible and appropriate, you link your benefits to their overall business strategy.

The questions that move the conversation from pain to gain are called Determine benefit questions because they ask customers to tell you how they will benefit from solving their problems. Instead of throwing your solutions at their problems, you ask them how they could profit from your solutions. As customers begin talking about the benefits of solving their problems, they start seeing you as the one who can alleviate their pain and provide them joy.

Examples of Determine benefit questions:

- → COMPUTER NETWORKS
  - If we did move ahead with this new backup system, how would it help your virus problem?
  - How would this relational database help your trend analysis?
  - Where might you allocate the funds saved by not paying overtime?

- → SALES TRAINING
  - Which products will your people sell when they access senior executives?
  - What do you think your customers will say when the sales effort is seen as more coordinated?
  - How will this type of training help you reach your strategic objectives?

- → OTHERS
  - How much would you put into the college fund if we cut your payments from $650 to $195/month?
  - If we could have the roll bar included, how might it address the safety issue?

Asking P.A.I.D. questions leads customers through the buying process. Research has found that customers begin thinking about buying when their PRESENT CIRCUMSTANCES change, often because a value trigger is pulled. They then follow a set of procedures, or subconscious rules, that help them process the AREAS OF CONCERN raised by the change in their situation. In larger purchases, these procedures may include a variety of tools to assess the I<small>MPACT</small> of their discomfort and devalue what they have. They decide to buy when they D<small>ETERMINE THE BENEFITS</small> you offer are greater than buying from your competitors or doing nothing.

In his superb book, *SPIN Selling,* author Neil Rackham, Ph.D., shows how top salespeople who ask questions in this manner produce dramatic increases in sales.[5] Dr. Rackham uses a slightly different set of questions, but they're similar to the P.A.I.D. approach described here. One group of 42 salespeople taught to use this questioning approach increased sales by 17% compared to the control group, which *decreased* sales by 13% due to a very competitive market. In another study described in his book, Rackham discovered that 27 of the 55 high-tech sales professionals who continued using their recently learned questioning skills increased sales by about 19%.

You too can increase your sales-call success by at least 20% by using this questioning approach during the diagnostic phase of your sales calls. Here's how a sales call might flow using P.A.I.D. questions with a senior manager:

You: Hello, Ms. Customer. Thank you for taking the time to see me. As you know, our team has been working with a few of your supervisors to get a better understanding of your current billing system and what might be needed in this area. They indicated that a more streamlined, user-friendly interface is what is most crucial to them. Is this what you feel is most important about a new system?

Ms. Customer: No, that's not my top priority. Our number one issue is reducing our accounts receivable (AR).

You: (Impact question) Oh, really? Do you mind if I ask why?

Ms. Customer: Because our AR is 30% higher than comparable companies.

You: (Impact question, NOT a benefit statement) How does that affect your bottom-line?

Ms. Customer: (avoiding your question) We won't have a bottom-line unless we get our AR in order! It's killing us. Unless we get more competitive, we're going to be eaten by the big boys down the street. What can your company do to help?

You: (summarizing, but dodging her question for now) I'll get to that in a second, if that's OK, Ms. Customer. Right now, I would like to make sure I understand your AR issue. If I hear you right, you want to decrease the AR to improve the bottom-line so you can be more competitive?

Ms. Customer: Exactly!

You: (Impact question) Ms. Customer, if you were able to decrease your AR by about 30%, what would you estimate would be your yearly savings?

Ms. Customer: About $90,000.

You: (summarizing): So you would be saving about $270,000 over the first three years if you decide to move ahead with a new system that reduced your AR?

Ms. Customer: Yes.

You: (Area of concern question. You know that the competition can claim cost-savings too, so you shift your questions to an area where you have a unique advantage.) How would you integrate the new billing system with your existing systems?

Ms. Customer: Oh, that's no problem. Our IT people will handle it.

You: (Impact question) I see. Are the IT people working on any other projects for you? (You know they are busy. You also have a unique product advantage in this area.)

Ms. Customer: Well…yes. They are working on the new ABC system.

You: (Impact question) Is that taking a fair amount of their time? (You know the answer because you did your homework.)

Ms. Customer: Yes, in fact it is taking a lot of their time and they still can't get it all done. We have to hire a few sub-contractors to help.

You: (Impact question) Is that costing a few dollars?

Ms. Customer: A few dollars! By the time it's all done, it will cost us more than $375,000 in total IT Department programming time to get the system integrated.

You: (Determine benefit question) If your new billing system eliminated the workload on your IT folks, so they could concentrate on your other priorities, how might that help?

Ms. Customer: When you put it that way, I guess it would be cost-effective to keep them focused on their other projects and priorities. Could you help us there?

You: (See below to learn how to "Earn Agreement" to take the next step)

Do you see how these P.A.I.D. questions helped you, *and this manager,* understand her circumstances, concerns, and the impact of these concerns? They moved her through the purchasing process, from awareness of an issue to asking you for your prescription. When you ask P.A.I.D. questions, you are combining the research on how customers make purchasing decisions with what science says is an effective questioning strategy.

Remember to ask these scientific questions with soul. *Be Real* by being true to who you are, and bringing your YOUniqueness to the call. If you love financial analysis and you think it's important to your customer, bring this strength to your call. If on the other hand you're more skilled using pictures to sell, that's what you should bring to the table. Recently, as I was teaching a group of consultants how to ask P.A.I.D. questions, one of them said he was not comfortable asking about pain. He felt it wasn't really who he was. Although I believe the research says we should ask Area of concern and Impact questions, I suggested that he honor his soul and ask mostly Present circumstance and Determine benefit questions.

You also honor your soul by *Being Present* with your customer as you ask these questions. It's easier to "be here" during the call when you prepare before the call. You don't want your cup to be so full of your own agenda that there isn't room for your customer. Write several questions before the call, and then follow a pre-call ritual to set the tone of being with the customer during the call. Adjust your style of questioning to suit this customer on this call. Noticing the details of their office and style can help you connect with them. You want them to be thinking, *friend,* when you come knocking on their cave.

Finally, *Be Deep* by doing your homework ahead of time. The more you know about your products and how they serve this customer, the more your customer will appreciate their time with you.

IV. PRESCRIBE — *Earn agreement to take the next step*
How would you like to shuffle into a doctor's office, only to have him prescribe a powerful treatment without asking you any questions? Would you swallow that pill? Neither will your customers. You earn the right to take the next step in the sales process (i.e., write a prescription) by asking P.A.I.D. questions first. Then and only then, like a doctor who conducts a thorough history and physical to accurately diagnose a patient's pain, have you earned the right to offer a prescription. Only then will your customer swallow your recommendation.

The diagnostic stage of the sales call ends when the customer tells you, in response to your Determine benefit questions, how your product could relieve their pain. Your customer is now happy to hear what you think the next step should be. Your prescription becomes as easy as making a recommendation. No sweating over closing. No memorizing 101 ways to close the sale. No looking for subtle signs to see if they're ready to close. And no agonizing over objections. Here is a simple four-step approach to writing a prescription for your customers:

1. Summarize the benefits they gave you in response to your Determine benefit questions

2. Ask if there is anything you missed or need to discuss

3. Recommend a next step

4. Ask if they agree or have a different step in mind

For example:

> You: (summarizing) Ms. Customer, let me see if I understand this, you want a new billing system that can reduce your AR and save you about $270,000 in the first three years? And it's important to integrate it into your current system without additional costs to your IT department? Do I have that right?
>
> Ms. Customer: Yes.
>
> You: Is there anything else we need to review today?
>
> Ms. Customer: No, I think that covers it.
>
> You: Ms. Customer, I think we at XYZ can help you in these areas. We have installed several of our new billing systems locally. Do you want to see one in action, or do you have another step you'd like to take?

How surprised will you be when you start booking more business because your sales call ends with a simple, straightforward prescription and not a tension-filled close?

Why Closing Hurts Sales

When we were buying equipment at UCLA, a salesperson once ended his demonstration by asking us, "If we could get you six of these machines at half price, how soon could you give us the purchase order?" Like the character in the movie *Taxi,* my brain screamed, *You talking to me? Are you closing me?* We politely thanked him for his time and told him we'd get back to him. We did. He didn't get our business.

The 100 healthcare managers interviewed as part of my research for this book also bristle at these closing lines. They told me their favorite salespeople never used techniques like that. No wonder other researchers also tell us that traditional closing doesn't work anymore.[6] Customers are sales savvy because they are assaulted by advertising messages all day. They are bombarded by telemarketing during dinner, swamped by TV and radio commercials, and saturated by newspaper and magazine advertising. Your customers have heard those old sales closes before and want to work with salespeople who have dropped them. They can smell a close coming a mile away. So, stop trying to close them, and start earning the customer's agreement to take the next step by writing a prescription. Your sales will take off and your sales-call objections will disappear.

Just Say "Know" to Objections

Objections are negative comments customers make when they disagree with statements salespeople offer. Most often, these rebuffs are in response to a feature or benefit the salesperson has described. When I first started selling, I was taught that objections were good for sales, that they indicated a customer's interest in my products, and that I needed to overcome them if I wanted to close the sale. Sound familiar?

Here's what you need to "know" about objections: Customers object because they don't agree with a statement, or don't like the direction the conversation is going, or believe the salesperson is mistaken. When a salesperson tries to overcome their objection customers resist even more, usually subconsciously. To me, even the term "overcoming objections" conjures up images of a huge asphalt-crushing machine steamrolling down the road, flattening all obstacles in its path.

The belief that objections are good for sales is still found in many sales books and training programs. Yet, as I surveyed the research on successful selling here's something else you might want to "know." I couldn't find anything that substantiated these claims. In fact, there is research indicating that as the number of objections increase during a call, sales-call success *decreases*.[7] You read that right. Sales-call success goes down as the number of objections goes up. These findings confirm the feelings I had when I listened to salespeople trying to overcome our objections when we were buying equipment.

The best way to handle objections is to prevent them by asking P.A.I.D. questions. (Grandma was right, an ounce of prevention is worth a pound of cure.) That's because Determine benefit questions ask customers to *tell you* how they will benefit. How can customers object when you're not saying anything they can object to? How can they resist if they are busy telling you how they'll enjoy your product?

This chapter began by reviewing the research that confirms that there is a predictable sequence of stages that customers follow when they buy. As you apply this science with your soul on each sales call, you will increase the probability that you will reach your sales goals. But there's no guarantee. You still need to know how to handle the word NO. Dr. Scott Peck was right when he opened his best-selling book, *The Road Less Traveled,* with these words, "Life is difficult."[8] The life of a salesperson is very difficult. Most salespeople could use a few more techniques to stay motivated as they travel their long and winding road. If you're among them, use the tools of feedback to keep you on track.

CHAPTER 8

Using Feedback to Stay Motivated All Day

The Nature of Feedback — Part I

Webster's Dictionary defines feedback as "the return to the point of origin of evaluative or corrective information." Feedback surrounds us. A market-based economy works because consumers give continuous feedback to producers. (To buy or not to buy is the feedback question of capitalism.) Feedback is also a critical factor in the theory of evolution. Survival of the fittest is really the ability of a species to adapt to its changing environment (i.e., responding to the feedback from its surroundings). That's *how* they survive. Without feedback, we too would die. The human body incorporates thousands of feedback mechanisms that keep us alive. And proper use of feedback is also how the best salespeople thrive.

Feedback keeps salespeople on-track as they pursue their sales goals. Salespeople give feedback to themselves, hear it from customers, and feel it from managers all day. This is why feedback is the third major variable in the S3 Equation. (*FIGURE 8.1*). The equation shows that feedback is influenced by two scientific tools (*Motivation and Systems*) and one soul principle (*Be Deep*). This chapter explains how to use the latest research on Motivation to increase your sales-call success.

FIGURE 8.1: Three Keys To Using Feedback

SALES GOAL = COMMITMENT	X	BELIEF	X	FEEDBACK
Sales-call tactic	*Value*	*Modeling*		*Motivation*
Selling strategy	*Role*	*Mastery*		*Systems*
Soul principle	*Real*	*Present*		*Deep*

Science Says Feedback is Feed Forward

Think about the last time you received praise for a job well done. How did it affect the job you *just completed?* It didn't, did it? Of course not. But it may have influenced your next task. That's because feedback is really feed forward. It affects future performance.

Of the 18 studies Professors Locke and Latham reviewed in their book, 17 reported that when feedback was combined with goal setting, it improved performance more than goal setting alone.[1] Professor Jay Kim from Ohio Sate University confirmed these findings in a study of 101 retail salespeople.[2] Managers in the high feedback group met with sales teams every 2 weeks for 12 weeks and provided information about their selling behavior, results, and goals. Managers in the low feedback group provided general goals and little feedback. Those receiving the most feedback, especially about their selling behavior, showed the biggest gain in sales.

When Professor Alan Dubinsky (College of Management at the Metropolitan State University) studied 174 medical salespeople, he and his co-researchers found that salespeople who were supervised by actively involved managers (i.e., they gave more feedback), performed better than those under a "hands-off" or "call-me-if-there's-trouble" manager.[3] Not only was the performance better under the "hands-on" managers, the salespeople in this group also had greater job satisfaction, supervisor satisfaction, and higher levels of commitment.

These researchers are not saying that managers need to be in the salesperson's face all the time. In fact, there's evidence that says the amount of feedback managers dispense should be adjusted to the individual needs of each salesperson.[4] Sales stars need less input than the struggling rookies.

What the research is telling you, and your manager, is to use daily feedback to stay on track to reach the sales goals.

Maintaining Motivation As You Sell Your Way Through the Day
Selling is the toughest job in the world. To become a sales star requires taking "the road less traveled." Many salespeople don't reach the top of the mountain (they take the low or easy road) because they can't handle the negative feedback they get all day, usually in the form of the word NO. How do you handle this negativity as you drive from call to call? The top salespeople I have worked with use positive feedback throughout the day. Please adapt the following "motorvational" techniques to keep yourself going, especially when the going gets tough.

1. TALK TO YOURSELF BEFORE THE CALL
What you say is what you get. In other words, the feedback you give to yourself and how you describe what happens to you influence what you receive. Our minister puts it this way, "Your description is your prescription." You can use this power of "self-talk" by spending a minute before each call declaring aloud your positive intentions for the call. As part of your pre-call ritual, park a short distance from your customer's office. Use the short walk to repeat positive affirmations to yourself. Here are six affirmations you might want to try to get you started:

→ I am serving this customer on this call by...

→ My customer will benefit from my services because...

→ I see myself helping this customer as I focus on their needs

→ I see this customer relaxed and open to my ideas

→ I hear them answering my great P.A.I.D. questions

→ I feel the joy of success as they agree to take the next step with me

2. Walk tall, feel better

How do you walk into your customer's place of business? I never even thought about it until I tried the following feedback exercise:

> Sit down and start thinking about something that is bothering you. It might be a lost sale, a problem at home, a health-related issue.... As you think about this problem, create the clear sounds, pictures, and feelings that accompany it. Let your whole body feel the burden and pain of this situation. Please put this book down for minute and use your imagination to feel this exercise *emotionally*.

> Now, how would you describe the position of your shoulders, head, and eyes? If you're like most people, your shoulders are slumped, your head is tilted forward, and your eyes are looking down.

> Next step: Please stand up. (Come on, humor me for a second and stand up.) Now, shake your legs and arms. Look up, walk across the room with your head up, shoulders back, and smile. How does that feel? Are you as down as you were before?

> *"Act as if it were impossible to fail."*
> —Dorthea Brande

Long before Dorthea Brande etched these words in her 1936 classic, *Wake Up and Live,* two giants of science observed that how you move affects how you feel.[5] In 1872 Charles Darwin wrote, "The free expression of an emotion intensifies it."[6] In 1890 William James, the father of modern psychology, presented the flip side when he penned these words, "Refuse to express a passion and it dies."[7] Recent research confirms that your motion is a feedback mechanism for your emotion.

Professor Carroll Izard, from the Department of Psychology at the University of Delaware, reviewed the large body of research on what is called "emotion activation."[8] Her three key conclusions are:

1. More than 30 studies confirm that facial muscles play a role in mood alteration.

2. Facial muscle contractions change cerebral blood flow and near-chemical activity.

3. Specific body postures elicit specific emotions.

If you want to feel better during a call, move better on the way to the call. Put a smile on your face, head up, shoulders back, and march confidently to your customer's door. Stride as if they would be crazy not to buy from you. Pretend you are Superman or Wonderwoman, here to save the day. (Is that a cape blowing in the wind behind you?) Maintain this positive posture throughout your call. Don't take my word for it. Try it and see if you feel better when you move better. The proof is in your performance, not these words.

3. ASK QUESTIONS AFTER THE CALL

A lot of salespeople beat themselves up when a call goes poorly. Don't be one of them. Negative self-talk hurts the next call. As I told a Wells Fargo Bank sales trainer recently, there is no failure, only feedback. It's only failure if you don't learn anything. Take a minute or two after every call to answer feedback questions like:

→ What went well?

→ What could I do differently next time?

→ How can I grow from this?

→ What are some possible next steps?

4. Reward yourself

Positive reinforcement is a great way to give yourself feedback. If the call was successful, meaning you earned agreement to take the next step, reward yourself. Here are three simple steps to creatively pat yourself on the back for a job well done:

1. Write a list of little things you enjoy

2. Pick one of these items as a reward after a successful call

3. Give yourself the reward as you replay the successful call in your imagination

For example, a few of my favorite things include: drinking a soda, taking a nap, reading inspiring books, biking in the mountains, walking my dog, eating yogurt, seeing great movies.... So, when a client called a few days ago confirming a large contract, I celebrated by biking in the mountains and taking a mid-afternoon nap. Very simple and rewarding.

When you pat yourself on the back, make sure you apply the four I's of positive feedback:

→ Immediate: Give the reward as closely to the behavior as possible

→ Intermittent: Reward yourself randomly, not every time

→ Important: Make sure the reward has motivational impact for you

→ Interesting: Brainstorm fun, little ways to reward yourself. Use variety, the spice of life, to keep it fresh

5. Apply Motorvational Tips From Those At The Top

Listed below are 14 tips sales stars employ to stay positive, especially when things seem negative. The list was created from the responses I received when I surveyed a few dozen top performers. Pick a few that could "motorvate" you. Test-drive them to see which ones work, especially when you feel you might be running on empty.

→ *Eat well.* Forget all the fad diets. If you go on a diet, you'll go off it. The first three letters of the word diet tell you all you need to know. Snack on fruit, bagels, and nutritionally balanced energy bars in your car. My favorite scientific, yet very practical, resource for health advice is *The UC Berkeley Wellness Newsletter.* (WellnessLetter.com) They offer the following general guidelines:

○ Eat high-fiber foods, such as fruits, vegetables, beans and whole grains

○ Consume more fish and nuts

○ Decrease your intake of sugary foods, like white bread and junk food

○ Cut back on animal fats, meats and fast food

→ *Exercise regularly.* A little daily exercise will do wonders for your attitude and weight. You don't have to become an Olympian. Top performers stay fit by doing something aerobic regularly, even if it's a quick power walk. One mile burns about 125 calories, whether you walk it in 20 minutes or run it in ten. There are 3,500 calories in one pound. You do the math. A mile a day melts the pounds away.

→ *Keep Good Company.* Limit the time you spend with those who are optimistically challenged. Spend more time with people who make you feel good about who you are.

→ *Keep Learning.* Top salespeople are lifelong learners. They take courses, read books, subscribe to their customers' magazines, go to motivational meetings, join professional associations, and listen to audio-programs between calls. Our customers, products, and environment are constantly changing. Spend an hour a day soaking up new information to stay current and positive. Father Anthony deMello teaches us that being a lifelong learner is deeper than what we learn formally, it is also about the spirit in which we approach our entire day. (www.demello.org) In his illuminating book titled, *Awareness,* this Jesuit priest writes, "The one thing you need most of all is the readiness to learn something new."[9] Stay motivated all day by being open to learning throughout the day.

↝ *Enjoy Hobbies.* Get away from selling on a regular basis. When you're at home, be at home. The word recreation comes from re-create. You'll be more motivated and creative if you engage in active leisure during your down time.

↝ *Get Rest.* Make sure you get the rest you need. Experts tell us we need 7–8 hours of sleep per night. Few of us get it. Take a 20-minute power nap mid-day. The late, great Green Bay Packers coach Vince Lombardi was right when he said, "Fatigue makes cowards of us all."

↝ *Ask positive questions.* Salespeople who have a hard time hearing the feedback word called NO usually ask themselves or others negative questions, such as: *Why does this always happen to me? Who screwed up this time? When are they ever going to buy from me?* All these questions are legitimate and negative because they lead to negative thoughts. Salespeople who handle rejection better tend to ask positive questions, such as: *How can I make sure this doesn't happen again? What can I learn from this? How can I take some action now to increase my chances of getting the next order?*

↝ *Turn off the TV.* Go for a five-minute pep walk and talk with a loved one or your pet. Focus only on positive events.

↝ *Tell Stories.* Start dinner at home by reading or telling a humorous or uplifting story. One salesperson says he reads from books like, *Chicken Soup for the Soul.*

↝ *Be Thankful.* Make a list of things you are thankful for once a week. When you lose a sale or get hammered by a manager, focus on what you have.

↝ *Review goals daily.* We move in the direction of the dominant images we place, or let others place, in our minds. A goal is your compass to keep you focused on the big picture. Your goal decreases the sting of those pinpricks you experience every day.

→ *Write positive affirmations.* Write a few of your favorite positive affirmations or quotations on 3x5 index cards. Keep them with you and repeat them out loud to yourself throughout the day.

→ *Listen to uplifting audio-programs in the car.* Invest the time and money to turn your car into your Rolling University.

→ *Read positive books before you go to bed.* Have something other than the nightly news dancing around your brain all night.

Section III

*Long-Term Strategies
to Keep Your Sales Growing*

CHAPTER 9

How to Add Consulting to Your Selling

Role Clarity Predicts Long-Term Sales Success

The previous chapters explained how to increase your sales-call success by strengthening Commitment, Belief, and Feedback via the tactics of *Value, Modeling,* and *Motivation.* You have also read how to apply the soul principles of *Being Real, Present,* and *Deep* as you use these well-researched tactics during the call. The remaining chapters offer advice on how to increase long-term sales success by growing your COMMITMENT, BELIEF, and FEEDBACK via the three scientific strategies of *Role, Mastery,* and *Systems* (*FIGURE 9.1*). Without a long-term focus, you risk becoming a flash-in-the-pan, a shooting star, instead of a shining star.

FIGURE 9.1: The S3 Equation for Long-term Success

SALES GOAL = COMMITMENT	X	BELIEF	X	FEEDBACK
Sales-call tactic	*Value*	*Modeling*		*Motivation*
Selling strategy	*Role*	*Mastery*		*Systems*
Soul principle	*Real*	*Present*		*Deep*

Professor Churchill and his colleagues conducted one of the classic sales studies of all time, an analysis of 409 separate research studies. They found that the top three keys to long-term sales success were[1]:

1. Role Clarity

2. Skills

3. Motivation

The strength of Role Clarity in predicting sales commitment and performance was also reported by Mark Johnston from Louisiana State University.[2] He and his fellow researchers found that newly hired sales-people who learned their roles well were less likely to quit when they encountered the numerous obstacles the selling profession offers. Additional evidence was reported by University of Kansas Professor Ronald Michaels, who noted that low Role Clarity correlated with low commitment and high stress in 215 experienced industrial salespeople.[3]

While much of this book is focused on providing the skills and motivation to increase sales, this chapter and the next discuss the two roles (consulting and team leader) customers need you to play in today's dynamic, competitive business environment.

Why You Are Not a Consultant

Did you notice that the title of this chapter is *How To Add Consulting to Your Selling,* not *How to BE a Consultant?* If you are going to play the role customers want you to play, it's important to understand the difference. Consulting authorities and authors Lippitt and Lippitt define consulting as "aiding an organization to mobilize internal and external resources to deal with their challenges."[4] Thus, while salespeople sell products or services to customers, consultants help customers apply internal resources to solve problems. Of course salespeople help too, but *how* they help is by selling what they have to people who need it. The first principle of soulful selling is *Be Real.* So don't pretend to be a consultant, be a salesperson who adds consulting to your selling.

When you add consulting to your selling, as described in this chapter, it announces to your customers that you are an expert in their business and that you care about what they care about. And when they see and hear how well informed you are about their priority issues, they will find you very persuasive. Remember, an analysis of 114 studies by Professors Wilson and Sherrell found that the number one predictor of persuasion was "perceived level of expertise."[5]

Follow the six steps described below to add consulting to your selling. You'll see that doing so not only builds your credibility, it also focuses customers on the value of your solutions, instead of the price of your products. Pricing objections will plummet and profit margins will soar because customers are willing to pay more for products and services which are directly linked to their critical business problems. As Robert Hershock, Corporate Vice President of Marketing for 3M, said: "You have to go beyond what your customer says to what is really needed. And what is really needed is added value…"[6]

The Six Steps of Adding Consulting to Your Selling
Fortunately, you are well on your way to understanding the consulting process because you already know how to develop P.A.I.D. questions, the fourth step in our approach. (*TABLE 9.1*) Asking P.A.I.D. questions unlocks customer value during the call. Following these six steps of adding consulting to selling is the long-term strategy to help you create value throughout the entire sales cycle.

TABLE 9.1: Adding Consulting To Selling

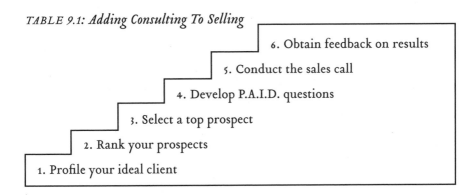

6. Obtain feedback on results
5. Conduct the sales call
4. Develop P.A.I.D. questions
3. Select a top prospect
2. Rank your prospects
1. Profile your ideal client

1. Profile Your Ideal Client

A marketing director once told me that her company treated all customers the same. I asked her if all their customers treated her company equally. When she smiled the answer no, I asked her how many of their 1,000 customers provided the highest margins, meaning those that were most profitable to her organization. She said she didn't know, but would find out. The next day she informed me that their top 200 customers gave them 80 percent of their business. I then asked her several questions about these "best customers." She couldn't answer them very well.

Professor Peter Drucker, whom the *Harvard Business Review* calls the father of modern management (www.peter-drucker.com), writes in his classic book, *Management Tasks, Responsibilities, Practices*, "that the aim of marketing is to know and understand the customer so well that the product or services fits him and sells itself."[7] The problem is that this marketing director, and many of her contemporaries, don't really know their customers well. Therefore, the salesperson (that would be you) is often left to answer strategic questions such as: Who are your high margin customers? What are their unique attributes or characteristics?

In their excellent book, *Strategic Selling,* Miller and Heiman explain the importance of these "win/win" customers.[8] They point out that understanding the characteristics of these "best" customers helps you identify which current customers provide the most opportunity for more business and what future customers (i.e., prospects) best fit your selling style, expertise, products and services.

These win/win or best customers provide the biggest bang for your buck because of the 80/20 rule, which says that 80 percent of your sales usually comes from about 20 percent of your clients. The 80/20 rule is why the marketing director found 200 of her 1000 clients generated 80 percent of her company's sales. Century 21 Real Estate knows the value of the 80/20 rule. Ken, one of their owner/brokers, told me about their program called the "Preferred Client Club." Agents sign their strategic clients up for the program. These clients then receive magazines, cards, and other mailers (50 pieces over a 5-year period) with the agent's name on the material. It keeps agents in touch with their best clients. The investment firm Charles Schwab answers its best clients' phone calls within 15 seconds. Others may wait for 10 minutes. The mutual-fund leader Fidelity uses the profitability of its clients as a means to tailor their offerings. The airlines covet frequent flyers, casinos cater to high rollers, and grocery stores take care of their frequent buyers. The best companies and salespeople identify who their best clients are, service them well, and fish for more prospects like them.

"One whale is worth a thousand minnows."

When I profiled my best clients during my Siemens selling years, I discovered that they were in large hospitals and academic medical centers, not the mid-size hospitals where many of my sales colleagues were most successful. My win/win clients tended to purchase larger computers and networks, cared about quality, and needed research capabilities. I had worked in the academic environment and therefore understood their issues. Selling to these clients was where I felt at ease, which allowed me to be more me, more real. My authentic self shone more brightly as I worked more with these clients and searched for more prospects like them. In other words, I sold with more soul when I focused on my strategic clients. I didn't ignore other prospects, I just spent more time looking for whales. In hindsight, it seems obvious that my sales would increase as I added consulting to my selling. But as Richard Farson says, "There is nothing as invisible as the obvious."

"Many salespeople fish for minnows While standing on whales."

The profiling process outlined below will help you identify the whales *for your territory and selling style.* These whales are your win/win, top 20 percent, strategic clients. The process begins by creating a chart illustrated in *TABLE 9.2.* Make your own chart using the table as your guide. Complete the chart by following these steps:

TABLE 9.2: Profile Your Ideal Clients

YES Clients	YES Characteristics	OH NO Clients	OH NO Characteristics	IDEAL Client Qualities

YES Clients: LIST YOUR TOP 5–10 CLIENTS. These are clients with whom you enjoy working and vice versa. They put a smile on your face when you think about them and when you make appointments to call on them. You may even feel some soul connection with them. These are your current win/win clients, who also deliver high life-time value to your company.

YES Characteristics: WRITE SEVERAL DEMOGRAPHIC AND PSYCHO-GRAPHIC CHARACTERISTICS OF YOUR YES CLIENTS. Demographics include things like their size, location, industry, number of locations, revenues, and so forth. An article in *Sloan Management Review* identified three keys to determine the lifetime value of clients: Margin (revenue minus cost of serving), Retention (probability of staying with you), and Discount Rate (current cost of capital).[9] Don't worry if you can't calculate all these numbers. Just use the concept to help "guesstimate" the demographics of your best clients. Psychographics are the less tangible but equally important *and* soulful characteristics. These include qualities such as integrity, trustworthiness, reputation in the industry, openness to new ideas and change, desire for stability, influence in the community or industry, value placed on relationships, emphasis on quality.

OH NO Clients: LIST FIVE OF THE WORST CLIENTS YOU EVER HAD IN THIS COLUMN. These are your "Oh No" clients because that's what you moaned whenever you had to deal with them. Maybe they always beat you up about price, or unfairly criticized your service, or whined about every minor problem. They were (or are) very costly clients in terms of time and money.

OH NO Characteristics: WHAT ARE THE DEMOGRAPHIC AND PSYCHO-GRAPHIC CHARACTERISTICS THAT MAKE THESE YOUR "OH NO" CLIENTS? My lousy clients had attributes such as: Low number of hospital beds, over-emphasis on price, remote region of my territory, poor attitudes, win-lose negotiation style, arrogant attitudes, and lack of loyalty.

IDEAL Client Qualities: WHAT CHARACTERISTICS BEST DESCRIBE AN IDEAL CLIENT? Review the *YES* and *OH NO* characteristics, and then write the top four qualities that define your win/win client. These are the characteristics you'll use to rank a list of prospects.

2. RANK YOUR PROSPECTS

Selling strategy is about deciding which prospects to focus on and which ones are too costly to pursue. In order to prioritize your prospects, create another chart following the format seen in *TABLE 9.3*. Write your top 10 prospects (or however many prospects you usually deal with in a month) in the left column of the chart. Now give each of these prospects a score ranging from -4 to +4 based on the characteristics you just identified for your ideal client. The prospects with the highest score are your target accounts, your whales. These are your top prospects.

TABLE 9.3: Rank Your Prospects

Prospect Name	Prospect Score

3. SELECT A TOP PROSPECT

Select a top prospect to call. If this is your first time through this process, select a prospect whom you feel comfortable calling. The art of Mastery teaches us to take small steps when beginning a new skill. The easier it is to take that first baby step, the easier it will be to take the next one. A body in motion tends to stay in motion.

4. DEVELOP P.A.I.D. QUESTIONS

Create several P.A.I.D. questions that focus on what's of high value to this prospect prior to the call. Professional consultants do not stop by just to say hello. They are held accountable for every minute they invest with their clients. You need to hold yourself accountable as you add consulting to your selling. The P.A.I.D. question approach summarized below serves as a reminder to help you focus on value during every sales call:

PRESENT CIRCUMSTANCES ⇢ How and what is your prospect doing now? Answer this question as completely as possible before your call. The number one predictor of persuasion is "perceived level of expertise."[5] In today's environment, that expertise is best demonstrated by understanding their business before you walk in. The more you are perceived as an expert in *their* business, the more they will be persuaded by your value proposition. Do your homework before you call: search the Internet, call your prospect's customers, review their situation with salespeople in your organization, contact customers in other departments within your prospect's organization, read their trade magazines and journals, and anything else that will you help understand their business.

When you call your prospect, you will have earned the right to open the call with a Present circumstance question, such as:

Your technologist told me she often stays late completing the analysis. So before we get started, could you help me understand why she needs to stay late?

AREA OF CONCERN ⇢ What is really bothering the prospect about their Present circumstances? Your focus needs to be on their pain, where it hurts, and what is triggering the possibility of buying. Write a few of these "irritation" questions where you have a competitive advantage. In the above example, if the prospect responded that her technologist stays late processing studies because of an over-loaded schedule, you might ask:

Is this overtime affecting your budget?

Impact of concerns ➙ Prepare "magnifying glass" questions to understand, and focus attention on, the high cost of their concerns. Impact questions help you and your prospects appreciate the ramifications of their problems. They also let prospects feel the pain of their business problems and begin to see you as the pain reliever. How well your products and services alleviate pain governs their perception of your value. In our example, if the prospect is concerned about the impact of overtime on her budget, an Impact question could be something like:

Do you mind if I ask how this overtime is affecting your other priorities?

Determine benefits ➙ Write a few questions that encourage your prospect to tell you how they will benefit from your products and services. Determine benefit questions take the focus off the pain by directing the client's attention toward the relief you offer. Instead of you listing the benefits for them, prepare a couple of questions that ask them to tell you how they will benefit. In our previous example, if the prospect informs you that she is not going to train her staff because the overtime has drained her budget this year, you might ask:

If you had a new system that decreased processing time by 50 percent, how would it affect your training budget?

Asking P.A.I.D. questions is critical to adding consulting to your selling. It's how to conduct the sales call. So do your homework ahead of time, pick the few areas where you know you can add the most value to these strategic prospects, create a list of questions, and take the next step.

5. Conduct the sales call.
Zig Ziglar says, "Anything worth doing is worth doing *wrong*…until you get it right." Nothing ventured, nothing gained. Make the call following the sales-call stages previously described. After prospects tell you how they will benefit from your service (because you asked Determine benefit questions), they are well on their way to becoming strategic clients.

6. OBTAIN FEEDBACK ON RESULTS

How often do you check in with your clients, especially your strategic ones? When I surveyed hospital administrators about their vendor interactions, one of their most frequent complaints was that salespeople disappear after the sale. The last step in adding consulting to your selling is to make sure your client is experiencing the benefits you sold them. In today's instant-access-to-information society, if you don't deliver on your promises everyone hears about it faster than you can say "Internet." The old adage "undersell and over-deliver," relates to the soul principle of *Be Deep,* and is more important than ever today. Plan a little time every week to check that your strategic clients are getting more than they paid for. When they tell you how happy they are, ask for referrals or request that they put their praise in writing.

Adding Consulting Grows the Soul

Adding consulting to your selling increases your sales over the long haul because it improves both parts of selling: the sales process and the salesperson. The process is improved because you are applying the science of purchasing as you focus on strategic prospects. The person is improved because you are also growing your soul by becoming more:

REAL → Don't pretend to be a consultant. You are a professional salesperson with products and services that help customers solve their problems. That's who the customer wants to connect with, not a phony person pretending to be something or someone he or she is not. Also, Being Real is easier when you focus on strategic customers whose interests are similar to yours. When the customer suits your style, the fit is better for everyone.

PRESENT → Be so prepared for the call that you can relax and be fully present with your customer. Sales trainer Tom Hopkins admonishes salespeople to Practice, Drill, and Rehearse (P, D, R). Paradoxically, the best salespeople are so well rehearsed that they are able to forget about most of their sales lines, and be with their clients. They get out of their own way and let the call follow a relaxed, P.A.I.D. questioning format. *I am HERE for you,* is what the soulful salesperson communicates beneath the surface.

DEEP ➝ Top consultants know who their strategic clients are. They profile these best clients and create hot prospect lists. They are experts in demonstrating and adding value to these win/win prospects. Use these steps to identify your strategic clients, learn all you can about their business, and serve them with your wealth of knowledge.

Customers want you to play the role of a consultant because they need experts to help them solve their difficult business issues. And adding consulting to your selling is one way to demonstrate your expertise. But you can't do it alone these days. There is too much to know about your customers and their needs, too many buyers influencing each sale, and too high a rate of customer turnover to develop deep relationships. You need to add a second role to your selling to help you serve your customer better and demonstrate your expertise more fully. You need to add another arrow to your quiver called teamwork.

CHAPTER 10

How to Add Teamwork to Your Selling

Is Relationship Selling Dead?
I lost the largest computer network sale of my career two years before I left Siemens. At the eleventh hour of this sale, I learned that my "soon-to-be-customer" was being influenced by one of his colleagues in another department. It seemed that my competitor had brought in a team of people who convinced my customer to link the purchase of his equipment (the network I was trying to sell) to his colleague's purchase in the other department. I scrambled the best I could. But it was too little, too late. If only I had called my sales colleague in the other division to learn what was going on, I'm sure WE would have made the sale. The pain of that lost sale started me thinking about team selling.

> *"Pain pushes, while wisdom pulls."*
> —Reverend Michael Beckwith

A year after I lost that sale, during my final year at Siemens, I booked the largest order our division ever received. I say I booked the order, but *I didn't make the sale.* It took me about a year to complete the sale, and I needed a team of colleagues to help me address the numerous issues that surfaced during this time. My teammates included: our division's Senior Vice President, our Vice President of Sales, the district and area sales managers, our Vice President of Financing, the local service manager, a physicist from the factory, several computer programmers and engineers, a facility planner, and a few vendors from whom we purchased various products. That's why I say I didn't make the sale, our team did.

These two sales, one lost and one closed, were my clues that traditional relationship selling was dying.

The idea that relationship selling might be obsolete went over like a lead balloon when I spoke to a group of Roche Diagnostics seasoned sales managers. Like many sales managers, these veterans of pharmaceutical sales insisted that excellent customer relationships were the key to higher sales. I asked them to show me their data. They had none. Where's *your* research? They demanded. I answered...

Twenty-five years ago, Professor Chase surveyed a large group of executives and found that these executives ranked their relationship with their sales representative as the most critical element of the vendor interaction. When the same survey was repeated recently, these business executives did not even rank the relationship with their sales representative as one of the top five elements.[1] There's my data. Here's an explanation.

Is relationship selling really dead? Maybe not dead, but in many industries, not all (such as those requiring only a few sales calls), it is on life support. Customers in many organizations don't consider *a* relationship with *a* salesperson as important as it once was. That's because customers these days:

1. Have less time to devote to relationships

2. Are under more competitive pressure to produce business results

3. Have business problems that are increasingly complex and interdependent

4. Require more committees and project teams to be involved in purchasing

5. Are experiencing high employee turnover

6. Have easier access to more information, thereby decreasing the salesperson's role in this area

So yes, the old relationship approach to selling in many sales environments is becoming extinct, but a new one is being born. The new relationship is not just between you and your customer; it is between you, your customer, and your company. Of course customers still care about you, but it's now in the context of your relationship with your organization and the business value you *and your organization* bring to their business. They need the collective wisdom of your team, with you as the team leader.

As a salesperson who is adding consulting to your selling, you there-fore need to add team leader to the role customers want you to play. This is your second role, another arrow in your quiver to help you hit your long-term sales goal. You probably don't need to bring a team to all your sales. Although I have no research to point to, my work with sales teams over the past several years suggests that you should only add team leader-ship to your most strategic sales. When you do bring in a team, make sure you avoid the common causes of team failure.

Why Teams Fail
There is a lot of team selling going on these days, and a lot of team failure. You probably already sell with others now. If you never do, skip this chapter. If so, how goes it? Does your team occasionally suffer from some of the common causes of team failure listed in *TABLE 10.1*? If not, you can skip the rest of this chapter too.

TABLE 10.1: Common Causes for Sales Team Failure

Turf wars	Unclear goals
Internal focus	Undefined roles
No team rewards	Too many members
Poor team leadership	Lack of accountability to team

To address these causes of team failure, we turn to researchers who have studied team success. Robert Trent (Professor of Management at Lehigh University) and Robert Jones (National Association of Purchasing

Management Professor at Michigan State University) investigated 107 cross-functional teams involved in purchasing.[2] They found these five keys to team success:

1. Availability of resources

2. Participation from suppliers

3. Effective team leadership

4. High level of decision-making authority

5. Commitment to team assignments

Professor Deborah Ancona and her colleagues at MIT studied 169 teams in a variety of companies to discover what made teams work.[3] They reported that teams possessing the following five characteristics achieved their goals most consistently:

1. EXTERNAL ACTIVITY ⇢ reached outside the team for information and resources

2. EXTENSIVE TIES ⇢ used connections inside and outside the organization

3. EXPANDABLE TIERS ⇢ adapted different roles for various team members

4. FLEXIBLE MEMBERSHIP ⇢ allowed team members to come and go as needed

5. MECHANISM FOR EXECUTION ⇢ had clear goals, norms, and member objectives

To apply the results of this team research to your team selling, let us take a quick look at two disciplines: systems thinking and project management. (Creative breakthroughs within a profession often begin outside that profession.) They may seem unrelated to teamwork or sales at first glance.

Yet, scratch their surface and I think you will agree that, as writer Marcel Proust said, "The voyage of discovery is not in seeking new landscapes but in having new eyes."

Several years ago, I learned to facilitate an extraordinary workshop on leadership based on Dr. Peter Koestenbaum's *Leadership Diamond.*[4] It was at this time that I became familiar with an aspect of leadership called systems thinking. Dr. Koestenbaum and his team at Quantum Leadership Solutions taught me that systems thinking deals with the big picture, the parts, and the relationships among the parts in a system. (www.pib.net) During this same period, I was also regularly teaching my two-day course on practical project management. Project management is an engineering discipline that describes how to pull a group of people together to accomplish a specific goal. After teaching systems thinking and project management for a few years it occurred to me that I could adapt the principles of both to help sales clients, like Roche Diagnostics, meet their team selling challenges (and many of the causes of team failure listed in *TABLE 10.1*). Thus was born the Systems Thinking Action Teams (S.T.A.T.) approach.

The S.T.A.T. approach is designed to help you bring the right people together for a brief period to focus on a strategic client. It is not intended to be used all the time or with all your customers. Think of it as a tool to stimulate the creative juices of key people toward achieving an important sale. That's why this will not replace relationship selling; it's a strategic tool to use only when you think a team will better address customer issues. Your role is that of the team leader.

Systems Thinking Action Teams Increase Strategic Sales
1. SELECT A STRATEGIC PROSPECT. Decide which top prospect you want to pursue. Use the S.T.A.T. approach only on strategic prospects or existing customers from whom you think you could obtain substantially more business. If you ranked your prospects and clients as discussed in Chapter Nine, review the list with your manager and, together, select one prospect based on their strategic value. Remember, energy directed by a unifying force is close to genius.

2. IDENTIFY THE STAKEHOLDERS. Brainstorm a list of individuals who might be affected by, or influential in, this sale. In project management, these are referred to as the stakeholders. You can think of them as temporary teammates. They often include people inside your own organization such as sales and service managers, other salespeople who call on this client, administrative staff, and service engineers. They may also include people outside your organization such as vendors, subcontractors, and consultants. From your brainstormed list, select 4 or 5 teammates who you feel could provide the most insight or help with this client. Review the short list with your manager. Then call each person and request his or her attendance at a single meeting to discuss a strategic customer. E-mail them an agenda and relevant information about the prospect before the meeting.

3. SET A S.M.A.R.T. GOAL. (Five minutes) Begin the team meeting by clarifying why this is a strategic prospect to you and your company. Then ask the team to establish a goal regarding this specific prospect. Write it on a flipchart, then tape it on the wall where everyone can see it. Make sure your goal follows the KISS principle (Keep It Simple, Salesperson) and S.M.A.R.T. guidelines. Remind your team that S.M.A.R.T., as it relates to *this* approach, is an acronym for:

SPECIFIC   = What are we shooting at?
             ("S" doesn't represent soul in this approach)

MEASURABLE = How will we know we reached the target?

ATTAINABLE = Is it within reach?

RESPONSIBLE = Who is on the team?

TIMED   = When will we get there?

An example of a S.M.A.R.T. goal from the Roche meeting is: *Our team will have the ABC physicians group sign an exclusive agreement to purchase our glucose monitoring system by July, next fiscal year.*

4. **COMMIT TO THE GOAL.** (Five minutes) Increase the team's buy-in to this goal by asking them to brainstorm as to the benefits of reaching it. Here's how: Give everyone a blank piece of paper and ask them to complete the following sentence in 60 seconds: This sale COULD be important because…Tell them to make a long list of reasons why this sale might help them or the company. Explain that quality does not count, only quantity. Inform them that they will not have to share their list with anyone. Announce that a prize will be given to the person who generates the most reasons in 60 seconds. After the 60 seconds of brainstorming on paper, facilitate a brief discussion about why this sale is important. Write several of their reasons on a flipchart. Tape it on the wall, next to the goal. The goal and this list will remind everyone throughout the entire meeting of what they are aiming at and why it's important.

5. **NAME THE PLAYERS.** (Five minutes) Brainstorm the various players in this account who could possibly influence this sale. These may include: the economic buyer who gives final approval to spend the money, technical buyers who often specify performance characteristics, user buyers who use the product and wield influence, coaches who help guide you from the inside, and other buyers who might affect the purchase or the players. Speculate about possible buying influences, such as customers at different locations, customers served by different divisions of your organization, those who know the prospect you are selling to, or colleagues who are not on this team but know the various players. Also, ask the team to brainstorm who they *don't* know. What players might be hidden from view? (I lost that large sale mentioned earlier because I missed a major influence that came out of the woodwork near the end of the sale.) Make sure you brainstorm; no processing, discussion, or evaluation of ideas.

6. **BRAINSTORM BELIEFS AND ASSUMPTIONS.** (Ten minutes) Encourage team members to brainstorm all their beliefs and assumptions about the prospect, goal, or anything else related to the sale. Inconspicuous beliefs and unstated assumptions act like blinders, shielding people from insights, inhibiting creative solutions, or torpedoing commitment to subsequent action steps. One of the best ways to remove these blinders is to surface them in a risk-free environment. Your primary job in this

brainstorming step is to unveil that which is hidden. Do not let the team discuss, process, or even try to understand what others say. Understanding is not important at this stage. (A group of sales managers completely shut down because one manager kept asking his teammates questions during this step.) Team members will not reveal cherished beliefs or veiled assumptions if they feel they'll need to defend, justify, or even explain them.

To stimulate ideas, ask the team to complete this sentence: *I believe… or I assume…* Anytime anyone says anything, write it on the flipchart. If it comes up, write it down. Assumptions and beliefs frequently concern issues related to: timing of the sale, attitudes of various managers and salespeople, importance (or lack of importance) of various prospects, problems with your company's products or services, internal politics (yours or the prospect's), unrealistic deadlines, competing priorities, bureaucratic rules…

7. DEVELOP P.A.I.D. QUESTIONS. (Ten minutes) What does your team know about this prospect's Present circumstances, Areas of concern, Impact of these concerns, and Determined benefits? Tell them what P.A.I.D. questions are and ask them to help you come up with a few. Again, brainstorm these ideas and write them on a flip chart. If someone says it, write it. The purpose of this step is to gain a broad perspective of your prospect's issues. Getting lots of input here is like taking a picture from many different angles — you see things better when you have a 360° view.

8. MIND-MAP THE TASKS. (Two minutes) This is the last brainstorming step. Ask each team member to draw a one-inch diameter circle in the middle of a blank page, and to write the name of the prospect in the middle of the circle. Now tell them that you will give them two minutes to brainstorm as many tasks or action steps as possible that could help you reach the S.M.A.R.T. goal. Urge them to keep their pens moving because quantity, not quality, counts. When they are done, give them a ten-minute break, during which you make a list of all their tasks on a flipchart and post it on the wall.

9. FIND LEVERAGED ACTION. (Twenty minutes) Explain to your team that leverage in a system is found by bringing the parts together at the margins. (The word *leverage* comes from the Latin word lever,

"akin to.") In sales, this means your team must now decide on a few creative actions that bring the various parts together. These parts often include the various stakeholders identified in step 2 of the S.T.A.T. Model. Tell your team that they need to find a creative combination of unique action steps that might generate explosive results. Ask them to answer this question: *What unique combination of actions could bring key players together that might help us reach our goal?* Many sales teams find it helpful to draw circles on a flipchart to represent the various players or parts, then discuss how to merge these circles at the margins.

As the team starts generating ideas, you will know that they have found real leveraged action by answering two questions: *Does the action seem straightforward? Does it have the potential to generate major progress toward the goal?* If either answer is no, you may have identified action worth taking, but it's probably not leveraged action.

Finding leverage is a creative activity that takes time and persistence. My experience has been that most teams need to be pushed, persuaded, and cajoled into discovering leverage. Many generate worthwhile ideas early in this step, but rarely are these ideas truly leveraged. When they find it, they will feel it. A surge of energy in the room will announce that the team has found a combination of actions that could produce explosive results. So don't be afraid to push them to come up with something even better. I've had teams get upset with me, say they're done, but my exhortations (and begging) helped them achieve breakthrough leverage just when they were at the end of their rope.

Below is a simple story of leverage in sales. It illustrates how to bring the parts (players, stakeholders, and actions) together where they have a common interest. The names have been changed to protect the guilty.

STAKEHOLDERS AND PLAYERS: THE PARTS

You: The local salesperson

Prospect (Peter): Economic buyer who is making a big decision within the year. He is very active in the local association. Your company frequently supports association meetings.

Your prospect's manager (Mat).

Customer (Cathy): A satisfied customer who lives in a different part of the country. She is active in the same organization as your prospect, but at the national level.

Your sales manager (Sam).

Your boss's manager (Bob): He knows Mat professionally.

THE LEVERAGED ACTION

If you followed the S.T.A.T. approach with your small team (you, your manager, and your manager's boss), you might have come up with the following leveraged action steps:

The team decides that Bob (your boss's manager) should call Mat (your prospect's manager) to see if there's anything Bob can do to advance the sale. The team also suggests that Bob ask a few questions about the local association Peter (your economic buyer) belongs to.

When Bob calls Mat, he finds out that Mat not only strongly supports the local association, but also has asked Peter (his subordinate and your prospect) to become more active at the national level. This confirms what had surfaced during step 6 of the S.T.A.T. process (uncovering beliefs and assumptions).

Bob then asks Mat if Mat would like your company to sponsor a local meeting in Peter's hometown, but with speakers from the national association. When Mat indicates he likes the idea (because it would help Peter get to know the top brass in the national association), Bob suggests that the local salesperson (you) work on the details with Peter. Mat agrees, and says he will even call Peter to encourage participation.

You then make a call to Cathy, a happy customer living in another part of the country. With your manager's blessing (and budget), you invite Cathy to speak at (and help plan) the meeting which your company is sponsoring. She agrees. You also tell her that you need to have Peter involved. Cathy says, no problem.

You call Peter, who is excited about the meeting, and you give him Cathy's telephone number and e-mail so they can start planning the meeting. Cathy and Peter become professional colleagues through this association.

The meeting goes as planned. And when Peter begins the formal purchasing process three months later, you recommend a visit to Cathy's organization to see your equipment in action. You book the order a few months later.

Leverage is usually found in the relationship among the parts. In our example, it was the relationship among the stakeholders and the customer players: Mat (your prospect's manager who wanted to increase association involvement at the national level), Bob (your boss's manager who knew Mat and has supported the association for years), and Cathy (an existing customer who is already active in that association). Systems thinking principles teach us that when you bring the parts of a system to work together in areas where they have a common interest, you create explosive results. As one AT&T executive put it, "harmony occurs where self interests meet."

10. CHART YOUR PROGRESS. End the meeting by thanking the team and telling them you will keep them informed about the progress you've made toward the sale. Also, remind them that you will contact each of them regarding any action step they have agreed to take.

Your final step is to list the leveraged tasks required to achieve your strategic goal. The Gantt Chart is a tool used by project managers to monitor the sequence of steps. It's a bar chart that plots the actual time each task takes against how long you planned for each step. The time planned is represented by the top row of boxes. As a task is completed, you fill in the boxes below that task. E-mail each team member a draft of the chart for his or her comments, highlighting the tasks that person will be performing, and ask if they have any questions. There are lots of variations to this Gantt chart. I worked with an organization a few weeks ago that only wanted the start date and end date for each task, no bars. (*FIGURE 10.1*) They adapted project management tools to their environment. You can too.

FIGURE 10.1: *Charting Sales Team Tasks*

Action Item List							
	Time to Complete	Owner	Support	Start Date	Due Date	% Complete	Comments

One final reminder: Use the S.T.A.T. approach only for your strategic accounts. Not all your customers need you to play the role of team leader. Relationship selling isn't entirely dead. One of the problems with team selling these days is that many people believe that it's all (we use teamwork in all our calls) or nothing (we never sell in teams). Yet most sales environments require both teamwork and individual action. As philosopher and business consultant Peter Koestenbaum writes, "The marriage of individualism with community is a consummate art form."[5]

So as you keep those relationships going, keep your eyes open for accounts which need a team to help solve their business problems. Then use this approach to help you bring the right people together, for short time, to achieve a strategic sale.

"The process of planning is more important than the plan."

The Paradox of Being Real and Playing the Role

John, one of my sales teammates, told me I often sounded too stuffy when I first started using strategic selling in my accounts. He was right. I was over-emphasizing the consulting side of sales, sounding too business-oriented, and forgetting the soulful side. John said I didn't sound like me and seemed too preoccupied with my agenda on the calls. (Interestingly, I think John went too far the other way. He frequently stopped in just to "touch base" with his customers. Although he was being real, he seldom had a business reason for being there.) John helped me strike the dynamic balance between what science said my roles were (i.e., adding consulting and teamwork to my selling), while maintaining my soulful side of selling (i.e., being real, present and deep).

If you think you might have some difficulty playing your new roles *and* being real, practice your new consulting/teamwork skills with sales colleagues who are very soulful. They are the ones who are most sensitive to sounding too business-like. It wasn't my business-oriented sales friends who told me I was acting too stuffy, it was John; someone who was strong where I was weak. Practice your new roles around people who, like canaries that signaled coal miners of deadly gases, can serve as your early warning signals. The art of *Mastery* will show you how to accomplish this, one step at a time.

CHAPTER 11

Mastery Says, *Sweat the Small Stuff*

Mastery: The Magic of Thinking Small Over the Long Haul

Imagine you're visiting a friend who has just moved to a new, upscale neighborhood with lots of cul de sacs. On the first morning of your visit, let's say you decide to go for a long walk. As you march down the street, hypnotized by rows of manicured lawns and driveways showcasing their latest SUVs, it dawns on you that you have no idea where you're going. Since you will be visiting for a few days, and enjoy your morning exercise, but don't like getting lost, you decide not to stray more than a few blocks from your friend's home. You end up walking several small laps around the neighborhood. The next day you feel more comfortable in your new territory, so you widen the "track" by walking a few blocks further from your friend's home (same distance and time, but fewer laps because of the wider radius). You continue expanding your comfort zone, until on the last day of your visit, you stride outside and boldly go wherever you want, for as long as you want.

Congratulations, you have just demonstrated the power of *Mastery*—the long-term strategy needed to hike the belief that you can reach your goals. The S3 Equation illustrates that while *Modeling* is the key to building self-efficacy on each sales call, *Mastery* is the method to keep this belief growing over the long haul. (*FIGURE 11.1*) *Mastery* means practicing small steps. It's about using a consistent approach to rehearsing your sales skills. The journey of a thousand miles begins with, *and is completed by,* one step at a time. It's how you expand your personal territory and increase sales. To practice the art of *Mastery* is to grow new skills by taking a little action every day. Researchers, top salespeople, and common sense have been telling us for years that when we compound our interest in small change over time, we get results...Big Time!

FIGURE 11.1: *Mastery Builds Belief Over Time*

SALES GOAL = COMMITMENT	X	BELIEF	X	FEEDBACK
Sales-call tactic	*Value*	*Modeling*		*Motivation*
Selling strategy	*Role*	*Mastery*		*Systems*
Soul principle	*Real*	*Present*		*Deep*

"Several studies document the relationship of self-efficacy to performance on a variety of tasks across dozens of domains."[1] Professor Berry is telling us that one of the best ways to strengthen our belief that we can reach our sales goals is by taking consistent, modest action toward those goals. Similar conclusions were reported by Professor Sexton and his colleagues in their excellent review of the critical nature of incremental victories when learning any new skill.[2] The findings in these reviews were corroborated by the extraordinary work by Dr. Bloom at the University of Chicago.[3] He investigated 120 of the America's very high achievers in six diverse professions (concert pianists, research mathematicians, neurologists, sculptors, Olympic swimmers, and tennis champions). He interviewed peak performers, along with their coaches, parents, and other family members in order to uncover the common elements of their exceptional accomplishments. Although he didn't include salespeople in this study, his four key findings apply to anyone who wants to master their craft and reach their long-term goals. These 120 top performers:

→ Viewed their early practice and performance activities as play

→ Maintained a strong commitment to excellence

→ Received strong, on-going encouragement from coaches in their chosen fields

→ Developed high commitment to increasingly complex learning and growing

All four of these keys are related to taking small steps over time. Dr. Bloom's 557-page encyclopedia of achievement is reminding us that we can only reach our destination by developing the discipline of *Mastery*.

The Seven Steps to Long-Term Success

The seven steps of *Mastery* described below show you how to systematically practice the sales skills you learn in this book or any other resource. Take these steps to expand your comfort zone and grow your sales over the long haul.

1. Select a sales skill you want to improve. Then write a S.M.A.R.T. goal for this skill. Focus on a small, relatively simple goal. It's easier to begin a journey when you know the probability of reaching the destination is high. For example, if you want to increase the number of Impact questions you ask during sales calls, your S.M.A.R.T. goal could be: *I will ask 5 Impact questions on every sales call next week.*

2. Learn as much as possible about this skill from the many Models available to you. Who could you call who does it well? What books or audio-programs can you digest? Are there seminars or workshops you can take? For example, to improve your Impact question strategy, you could ask a few of the top salespeople in your company how they use these questions, which ones work best, and why. You could also read parts of the book, *Spin Selling*. Remember the mountain story? John found his way down the mountain because he learned how to take baby steps from his Uncle George.

3. Choose a method (or person) to provide feedback as you test your new skill. In other words, decide how to measure your progress. If you are fortunate enough to make sales calls with colleagues or managers, ask them to count your Impact questions during a sales call. If you are on your own, write a few Impact questions on a notepad as part of your sales-call ritual. Then, during the call, put a checkmark on your notepad each time you ask an Impact question. That which gets recorded gets repeated. Count what counts.

4. Apply the skill in a safe environment. Controlling fear, uncertainty, or doubt is what this step is all about. John found his way off that Wyoming mountain because of all the short, safe hikes he stumbled through during his vacations in Vermont. Safe environments are the training wheels of new skills. Olympic gymnasts practice new skills in safety harnesses. When you first try your new skill, do it where you feel safe and where the consequences of poor performance are minimal. Practice your new skill in the car, at home, with a friend. (I bought my first video camera so I could practice my sales presentations at home.) Try your small step with a low risk prospect or customer. Some salespeople attempt the new skill where they have little chance of closing the sale, others are more comfortable taking their training wheels off in front of established customers. Decide what works for you. Then do it.

5. Record feedback after using the skill. It's important to analyze your performance immediately after trying your new skill. Use the "sandwich technique." Begin your evaluation process by describing what went well. Make a quick list of things that you felt good about as you attempted this new skill. Next, write a few thoughts about what did not go as planned. Why didn't it? What can you learn from the trial that will help the next time you use it? Be gentle with yourself. Don't let your thoughts spiral you into the big, black abyss. Complete this step by refocusing on the positive.

6. Reward yourself for taking action. As discussed in Chapter Eight, using positive feedback can keep you motivated and on track throughout the day. When a baby learns to walk, the smiling faces of cheering adults spur the child on as it gains mastery over its environment. Employ the power of immediate rewards to reinforce your baby steps toward long-term success. These pat-yourself-on-the-back rewards increase the probability that you'll try, try, try again, especially if at first you didn't succeed.

7. Make this new skill a habit. Incorporate this skill into your everyday selling by using the habit of highly successful salespeople described in the next section.

"Sow a thought, reap an action,
Sow an action, reap a habit,
Sow a habit, reap a character,
Sow a character, reap a destiny."
—CHARLES READE, *1800's English novelist*

The Habit of Highly Successful Salespeople

In his best-selling book, *The 7 Habits of Highly Effective People,* Stephen Covey (www.franklincovey.com) writes that in order to create a positive habit, we need knowledge (what to do), desire (want to do), and skill (how to do it).[4] My experience with good, *not* excellent, salespeople is that they often excel in acquiring the knowledge and developing the desire, but have a hard time consistently performing the skill. In other words, good salespeople often don't know how to turn their knowledge and desire into a reliable skill.

Highly successful salespeople, on the other hand, understand that long-term success is built by turning daily actions into life-long habits. They know that knowledge is not power, only *applied knowledge is power.* (If knowledge were power, people wouldn't smoke, drink and drive, or be afraid to cold call.) Thus, a critical habit of highly successful salespeople is that they have learned how to create positive habits.

"First we make our habits, then they make us."
—JOHN DRYDEN, *1600's English poet*

The key to implementing new habits into your everyday sales life is to link the new habit to something you are already doing. In other words, you connect the new skill you want to become a habit to an existing habit. *FIGURE 11.2* expresses the concept in a simple equation.

FIGURE 11.2: Making New Habits

OLD HABIT + NEW SKILL = IMPLEMENTATION

I mentioned earlier that one of the powerful communication skills I learned was to adjust my style to match the customer's style. When I decided to apply this new skill during my sales calls, I wrote the letters NLP at the top of my sales-call notepad as a reminder to adjust my style. Every time I looked down to scratch a note during the call I saw the letters NLP. This prompted me to practice the new skill. After several weeks, matching became a habit. I had combined an existing habit (taking notes during the call) with the new sales skill (matching my customer's communication style) to implement a new habit (automatically adjusting my style during sales calls).

This concept is as old as tying a string around your finger. The only question is, how will you use the principle to help you practice the art of *Mastery?* Listed below are several examples of how highly successful salespeople combine their old habits with new sales skills. Adapt them to your selling situation and preferences. Then use them to create habits for those skills you want to master.

1. INDEX CARDS. Write a skill on a 3 x 5 index card. Put the card in your appointment book, pocket, or something you touch throughout the day. Whenever you pull out your appointment book, read the card. Put a check mark on the card every time you practice the skill.

2. POCKET CHANGE. Put seven coins in the right pocket of your slacks. Every time you put your hand in your right pocket, move one coin from the right pocket to the left pocket and remind yourself to practice your new skill. Let the coins be a metaphor about the importance of making small change over time. (Thanks to my friend and professional speaker Bonnie Dean for this suggestion.)

3. WATCH. Program your watch to beep on the hour. Use the beep to remind yourself to practice the new skill.

4. CROSS YOUR FINGERS. Visualize yourself using your new tool as you cross your little finger (pinky) with the ring finger next to it. Visualize the new sales skill when you review your morning goals and during your pre-call ritual. Create the rich mental images, sounds, and feelings as you imagine yourself successfully using the new tool. When you're actually face-to-face selling, cross your fingers as the reminder to practice what you imagined.

5. MIRROR. Slightly tilt the rearview mirror in your car. Every time you look in the mirror, tell yourself aloud how you are applying your skill today.

6. NOTEPAD. Write a "reminder word" at the top of the notepad you use during your sales calls. Just as in my NLP example, every time you looked down to scratch a note, you will be prompted to use your new tool.

7. APPOINTMENT BOOK. As you review your daily appointments in the morning, write a word or two in your Daytimer, PalmPilot, or whatever tool you use to organize your time, to remind yourself to practice your new skill.

8. PHONE. Since you probably use your phone a lot, write a post-it-note to prod yourself to practice the new tool whenever you're on the phone.

9. COMPUTER. How can you change your screensaver or scheduling software to inspire you to practice a sales skill? How about a post-it-note on your computer?

10. TEAM MEMBER. Who can you count on to regularly encourage you to take daily action toward your long-term goal?

These suggestions will help you master the habit of highly successful salespeople — the habit of making habits.

*"If you improve 1% per day,
in 70 days you're twice as good."*

—ALAN WEISS

How to Manage the Paradox of Mastering Skills and Being Present
An old coach of mine was fond of saying that his job was to teach players to "act reflexively." He said you wouldn't have time to think when you were under stress, only to react, and that your reactions would be based on ingrained habits. This same principle is true in sales, and is one of the reasons you should create successful sales habits. However, it's important not to lose your soul as you practice your skills.

One salesperson I used to know practiced his sales skills all the time. But he became so rehearsed that he sounded like a robot. His customers said they didn't buy from him because he came across as too artificial, too rehearsed, too "salesy." He lost the soul of selling because he over-practiced the science of *Mastery*.

The key to using your well-practiced skills without becoming too robotic during the call is to *Be Present* AS you use your skills. This requires that you manage the dynamic balance between being well prepared and being truly present with your customers. Your sales skills must be so well rehearsed that you become almost unconscious of them. I say almost, because if you are completely unconscious (i.e., all reflex and no thinking), you'll sound like a character out of the movie, *Stepford Wives*—a robot with no soul. On the other hand, if you over-focus on the Zen approach of only *Being Present* in the moment, you won't be practicing the seven steps of *Mastery*.

Here are a few keys to help you manage the dynamic balance between practicing new sales skills on customers and *Being Present* with them:

1. Brainstorm all the negative consequences that could occur if you over-focused on mastering new skills, but didn't pay attention to *Being Present* with your customer. Think about what would happen, how would you sound, what would the customer do if you came across like a machine? You might even brainstorm a list with your

sales colleagues or manager. Don't analyze, process, or judge what comes up, just write it down.

2. Brainstorm all the possible negative consequences that might occur if you only focused on *Being Present* with your customers, but didn't practice any new skills. What could happen if you waltzed in with no sales plan, no agenda, and no new tools to help move the sales forward? This is brainstorming. So, if it comes up, write it down.

3. Identify early warnings that could help you detect your over-focus at either extreme (too much rehearsing or only *Being Present*). Review your list of negative consequences, and then decide which of these would be triggered first. It is important that these early warning signals be able to alert you before it's too late. Canaries gave coal miners time to escape. Your signals also need to provide early response capability.

These three steps should help you avoid some of the problems salespeople have when they practice the science of *Mastery*. One manager tells his salespeople to continue rehearsing new stuff, but to forget about it when they are with their customer. He says that their practice sessions eventually seep into the call, but in a more natural manner if they don't worry about the skill during the call. See what works for you. You need to find your own dynamic balance between the science (i.e., increasing self-efficacy through *Mastery*) and soul (i.e., *Be Present*) of belief.

Managing that balance between *Mastery* and *Being Present* is analogous to sailing a small boat on windy day. If the wind grabs your sails and starts tipping you over, you need to jump to the other side of the boat and hang over the edge to maintain balance and keep moving. Sailors don't hope the wind stops blowing or lower their sails. So, don't stop practicing new skills; be more present during the call. That is how to manage the tension between the science and soul of believing as you increase your long-term sales.

CHAPTER 12

Systems of Feedback Keep You On Track

The Nature of Feedback: Part II

Chapter Eight explained that feedback is "information returned to the source." It showed you how to use short-term feedback to stay on track as you pursue your daily sales goals. The S3 Equation (*FIGURE 12.1*) illustrates that feedback is also influenced by a long-term strategy called Systems. This chapter explains what Systems are and how to use them to keep you on track toward long-term sales success.

FIGURE 12.1: The Systems of Feedback

SALES GOAL = COMMITMENT	X	BELIEF	X	FEEDBACK
Sales-call tactic	*Value*	*Modeling*		*Motivation*
Selling strategy	*Role*	*Mastery*		*Systems*
Soul principle	*Real*	*Present*		*Deep*

Sell to Your Customers, Not to the Plan

The commission plan is a feedback system salespeople deal with all the time. The plan is really a mechanism to give salespeople feedback regarding achieving specific sales goals. It is management's method of rewarding salespeople. It is also one of the most controversial aspects of selling.

Many salespeople don't consider the commission plan merely a reward system. They often see it as a manipulative tool, pushing them to sell products based on management objectives, rather than their customers' needs. Yet in management's defense, the plan must consider a variety of factors (budgets, market forces, shareholders' interests, sales managers' needs, production schedules, service quality). Many of these so-called "stakeholders" have their own competing, often contradictory, agendas. Pleasing everybody is Mission Impossible. How should a salesperson handle this omnipresent system of feedback called the commission plan? Deb has a clue…

> Deb was the top salesperson at MDS, the medical computer company where I had worked as an application specialist before joining Siemens. Deb had an outstanding reputation, as did MDS. Unfortunately, due to its inability to be innovative in a rapidly changing market, the company lost its edge, its market share plummeted, and it found itself going out of business.
>
> To fend off creditors during its final six months, the company increased commissions four-fold and cut prices in half. Talk about feedback and incentives! Salespeople made tons of cold calls and raked in piles of money during this "fire sale." Deb made lots of calls too, yet her income didn't go up, it went up in smoke.
>
> Deb refused to be seduced by the lucrative new compensation plan. She called all the customers who had bought from her during the last year (they were still under warranty), and encouraged them to return the products to the company. She told them she was worried about the service they would get and the impact poor service could have on their patients and business.
>
> When management heard what she was doing, she was fired. Her approach to this "fire sale" cost her big bucks and her job.
>
> You can probably figure out the rest of her story. She went on to become a sales superstar with another company. Her reputation for integrity followed her. So did many of her customers.

While this true story may seem a little extreme, it illustrates the spirit in which many top salespeople systematically approach their commission plan. They read it, stuff it in their files, and for the most part, forget about it. Peak professional salespeople sell to their customers, not to their company's plan. Their primary focus is on meeting the needs of customers, not the factory, or even their managers. Don't you know salespeople who occasionally pay so much attention to *what* they get paid that they forget *why* they get paid? Deb's story is a reminder that customer's needs, not the commission plan or incentive contest, should drive long-term sales strategy.

Does this mean you should totally ignore the commission plan? It depends. For example, one Fortune 500 company lost their top salesperson because of a poorly structured plan. He told me that the year he was the number one salesperson, a colleague who was number one in the same division but selling different products sold half as much as he did and brought in half the margins. However, this colleague earned twice the commission. (Imagine selling twice as much at twice the margin and earning half the commission!) He said he tried to talk with management about this inequity, but they wouldn't even listen. They kept telling him about their need to keep one of the company's production lines going. So, when a better offer came along, the commission plan's "long-term feedback" helped him decide to leave. Over the next few years, several of his sales colleagues left too. This company's division, once ranked at the top in market share, found its sales dropping like an anchor.

You may not be able, or desire, to handle your commission plan like Deb or this salesman did. That's not the point. The point is to sell to your customer, not to the plan. Letting your customer's needs drive your sales *is the best plan* for long-term sales success. When you do the right thing for your customer, the soul principle of *Be Deep* guarantees your long-term compensation. That's because the law of sowing and reaping is as reliable as the four seasons. Since we all spring from the same well, your compensation is assured over the long haul. It may not be in the form or time frame you expect, but the law of compensation will eventually prevail, just like gravity. And like gravity, this law is always at work whether you know it, like it, or use it.

"God may be slow, but He's never late."

How to Lose a Sale
A very good salesperson named Tom recently told me that his newly hired manager accused him of being negative whenever he tried to discuss his lost orders. Now, Tom just happens to be one of the most optimistic salespeople around. But he became so frustrated at not being able to "learn" from lost orders that, after six years of great sales, he accepted an offer from another company. He says his new company allows him to discuss and learn from lost orders.

Every salesperson loses sales, but few know how to do it well. In fact, salespeople rarely speak about loss. We are taught to have a positive mental attitude, be upbeat, wipe off the dust and grit of the journey and move on, and make another call immediately. To which I say, fine. It's fine to put a positive spin on a negative event. But too much spin makes us dizzy, especially if there are lessons to be learned in the loss. And a lost sale is often a teacher dressed in pain.

Processing lost sales is the second *System* of feedback that heavily influences salespeople. Yet most salespeople don't have a long-term strategy for handling it effectively. Fortunately, there is a method that allows you to both honor your soul's need to sit in the swamp of loss *and* meet the business's requirements to keep sales growing. So, next time the big one gets away, adapt the lost order *System* outlined below to fit your style and situation. You don't need to follow it for every lost order, just the ones that hurt and the ones you feel have lessons to reveal.

"Pain is a given, suffering is a choice."

1. DON'T JUST DO SOMETHING, SIT THERE.
In his book, *The Seven Storey Mountain,* Thomas Merton writes about the agonizing experience of watching his father die of cancer.[1] He says he learned the most powerful lesson about pain—the only way through the pain is through the pain. Having lost my mother to the same disease not long ago, I think Merton is right—the first step in dealing with loss is to

let the pain have its way with you. In time, you will be ready to move on. But first, you must mourn. Your soul needs to be with the pain of loss before you can get over that loss, especially when it's the big one that gets away. This mourning may mean taking some time away from selling. The amount of time off should be proportional to the value you placed on the order. I often took a day to sulk after losing orders that meant a lot to me. It doesn't really matter what you do with your time off, only that you take it.

As I write these words, Easter is on the horizon. The Christian religion teaches that Christ rose from the dead after being crucified. But he only ascended after he spent three days in a sealed cave. Whether you believe in the teaching or not, you can think of his three days in the darkness as a metaphor for what we all need to do when we experience loss. We all need time in the darkness, time to be still, time to reflect. The new day will dawn, but only after the night. Your cave is the start of your re-birth, your "resurrection."

Why do we need the dark? I think it's because at night, it's easier to see our light. And contrast is how we see.

So, when you lose an order, sit in the stillness of the swamp for a while. Your soul needs to be with the pain at night before it can gain the right insight.

2. WRITE FOR INSIGHT.

Your AM Pages become your "mourning" pages for a short time. Your intuition isn't easily heard amid the clamoring noise of sales. Your still, small voice may have something to whisper in the silence. So wake up and write three pages of nonstop, brain dump stuff. Don't think, don't process, and don't force anything. Just write three pages of fast, flash, first thoughts. Have faith you will hear what you need to hear. Let your inner voice have a voice. Don't worry about what spills out. You need an outlet for the frustration, anger, or steam that may be seething below the surface. Use your writing to release and let go of any emotional pressure. Here are a few ways to jump-start your writing:

→ This hurts…

→ In my darkest hour…

→ The pain of birth teaches…

→ I have grown through adversity by…

→ Lessons I have learned the hard way…

3. LESSONS LEARNED REPORT

After grieving and reflecting, it's time to concentrate on what you learned and will do differently because of the lost order. Remember, Dr. Hilman defined the soul as that which "makes the meaning out of experience."[2] Lost orders can be learning experiences if you choose to look for meaning. The attribution theory in psychology teaches us that making meaning out of what happened in the past influences the future. Therefore, within a week of your loss write a brief report on the lessons learned. A quick way to do this is to take a blank sheet of paper and draw a line right down the middle. Title the left column, *Went Well.* Title the right column, *Do Differently.* Next, brainstorm a list of all the things you feel went well during this sale (on the left side). I know you lost the order, but that doesn't mean some things didn't go well. Then write a list of all the things that you will do differently because of this lost order on the right side. What will you do more or less of? What could you do better next time? Just brainstorm and let your ideas flow. The whole purpose of this step is to direct your attention on how to use the lessons of this sale to help future sales. (It may also help you fill out the lost order form.)

4. DON'T JUST SIT THERE, DO SOMETHING.

I once collaborated on a very large sale with a colleague, Tina. If we booked it, we both would earn a big commission check. We lost it. Ouch! We were both devastated. A year of blood, sweat, and…beers. Nothing to show for it now except a lost order form. I mourned the loss by taking a couple days off and biking in the mountains. Tina mourned the loss by riding her horse. I re-focused on my sales goals, and had a good year.

Tina never recovered. Whenever I saw her, she talked about the "big one that got away." After two years of missing her quotas, she was fired.

Tina's inability to grow her soul can explain what happened. As you may recall, one of the "Cs" of the soul principle *Be Deep* is to understand the "Cause" of happiness. Remember the happiness equation (Happiness = Experience − Expectations)? Do you see how it predicts Tina's misery? Prior to the sale, she had high expectations. (Let's give her expectations a score of 9.) She then had the experience of losing the sale. (Let's give her negative experience a score of -9.) You do the math. (−18 = −9 −9) No wonder she was miserable! I was too! But the major point here was that she stayed miserable because of her inability to let go of high expectations and her ineffectiveness in learning from the experience. While she subconsciously stayed a minus 18 after the sale, I chose to let go of my expectations and learn my lessons.

Don't let what happened to Tina happen to you. Follow the system outlined here to put the happiness equation to work for you. Keep your high expectations of making the sale. However, let go of these expectations when you lose one. Remember that lost sales don't make you miserable, your attachment to them does. Perhaps this is why Peter Drucker says we often fail because of what we hold onto. And maybe this is why best-selling author and lecturer Dr. Wayne Dyer observes that one of the traits he sees in highly functioning people is their uncanny ability to shut out the negative past.[3]

Try using the feedback system described here to help you see your "negative" sales experiences in a positive light. Take time off, lick your wounds, and learn your lessons from lost sales. Then stop complaining, refocus on your goals, and get back in the saddle again.

"We mourn with tears, we honor with action."

Ask Yourself Positive Questions

Another one of the "Cs" of being a deep salesperson is Choice. Whether salespeople feel good or bad about what happens to them is not a matter of chance, it's a matter of choice. The happiness equation is really all about choosing to let go of attachments and choosing to see the positive in the seemingly negative. And one of the best ways to make positive choices over the long haul is to have a systematic approach of asking positive questions.

When "bad" things happen to you, do you have a bad habit (i.e., negative system) of asking questions like: *Why me? How did I mess this one up?* Or *When am I ever going to get it right?* We all ask these questions at various times. It's normal to be hard on yourself for a short time, especially when you make mistakes. How often do you hear questions like these around the office, home, or in your head?

→ When is my manager going to help me with this?

→ How come our engineers can't get it right?

→ Why are my customers so hung-up on this problem?

→ Where's our team service when you need them?

→ Why do I have to spend so much time doing paperwork?

→ Why can't marketing give us what we need?

→ Who messed this up?

→ How come I ask so many negative questions?

All these questions are negative because they lead to victim thinking. They suck us into the dark abyss of the "woe is me" mindset. Instead of helping us fix the problem or learn a lesson, the "negative questions" seduce us into pointing fingers and assigning the blame. Asking negative questions limits our options, because like an ostrich with its head in the sand, our view of the world becomes limited. Negative questions may feel good in the moment, yet over the long haul they leave us stuck in the muck because they don't lead to productive action.

Positive questions do the opposite of negative questions. Positive questions focus on action and personal responsibility. Positive questions move us from victim thinking to meaningful activity. They encourage us to pull our head out of the sand, and see more options. Creating a *System* of questions to help us handle the adversity inherent in selling leads to long-term success. Here are those negative questions turned into positive questions:

→ How can I get my manager to see how important this is?

→ How could my customers show our engineers a better way?

→ What could I do to answer my customer's concern about this issue?

→ What do I need to do to convince service we need them in this account?

→ How can I spend less time doing paperwork?

→ What can I do to help marketing meet our needs?

→ How can I make sure this doesn't get messed up again?

Do you see and feel how these questions lift us out of sinking thinking into possibility thinking? When we take our heads out of the sand, the view is better and the options more abundant. It's fine to ask a few negative questions when we are hammered by one of selling's many difficult circumstances. It's natural, it's human, and it's soulful to sit in the swamp for a while. As Thomas Moore writes, "We become persons through dangerous experiences of darkness."[4] But sales stars don't moan and groan for long. They rely on a *System* of positive questions to increase long-term sales success because they understand that positive questions increase their choices. In his wonderful book, *The Questions Behind The Questions,* John Miller describes how to create a *System* of asking positive questions.[5] I've adapted his approach to fit sales. Please adapt the one outlined below to suite your selling style and environment:

1. Make a list of the things that bug you most in sales (e.g., lost sales, poor service, inadequate commission plan, too much paperwork...)

2. Write the negative questions (that's right, NEGATIVE questions) you sometimes ask when these things happen

3. Rewrite these negative questions into positive questions by following these simple guidelines:

   →‣ Start with *What* or *How*

   →‣ Focus on you

   →‣ Advocate action

   →‣ Embrace the spirit of personal responsibility and accountability

4. Keep a list of these positive questions with you (e.g., 3 x 5 index cards, appointment book, PDA, post-it-notes…) to review anytime you feel yourself slipping into the deep, dark abyss of sinking thinking. Here are a few examples of "generic" positive questions to keep on hand:

   →‣ How critical will this seem five years from now?

   →‣ What could be funny about this down the road?

   →‣ Who can help me?

   →‣ What does this irritation tell me about me?

   →‣ What unrealistic expectations did I have?

   →‣ How do I choose to see this in a different way?

   →‣ How can I shine my God-given talents in this darkness?

   →‣ What positive questions could I ask myself to feel better right now?

Managing the commission plan, losing sales successfully, and asking positive questions are three *Systems* of feedback that will keep you on track as you pursue your long-term sales goals. But you probably won't reach the top in selling unless you know how to call on top executives.

"What is to give light must endure burning."
—Victor Frankl

CHAPTER 13

How To Sell To Top Executives

Calling at the Top to Increase Sales

A consultant friend of mine, Alan, received a call from Tom, an HR manager, who said his company was growing so fast that they needed to improve their interviewing and hiring skills. When Alan asked who approved the budget for the training, Tom said his boss (a Vice President) did. Alan explained that he always likes to touch base with the person who is funding the training (i.e., economic buyer), and asked the HR manager if he could set up a conference call with the VP. Well, Tom hemmed and hawed about how busy his boss was and said that Alan should just submit a training proposal. When Alan finally convinced him that the call would only take a few minutes, Tom gave Alan the VP's number. The VP informed Alan that the CEO had already hired his cousin to improve the staff's interviewing skills. He said they didn't need Alan's training.

Of course he was disappointed not to work with them. However, the moral of the story is that Alan didn't waste any time interviewing people about their needs or putting together proposals. He had just saved an enormous amount of time. In most sales, especially large or complex ones, there are many customers influencing the sale, but only one person writing the check—the economic buyer. Everyone has his or her input, but the economic buyer has the money. This chapter shows you how to reach the top of the selling profession by calling on top executives, like Alan's economic buyer. Here's why selling well at the top is critical to your long-term success:

1. INCREASES YOUR PRODUCTIVITY

How many hours do you waste chasing sales that never happen? You know, the ones where the customer doesn't buy at all, ever! In his book, *Selling To The Top,* David Peoples reports that productivity increases when you call at the top because approximately 30 percent of all potential sales end up with no sales.[1] Top executives can give you the inside scoop on many of these "phantom" sales, most of which are never real selling opportunities in the first place. Often they are the product of some manager's imagination, supervisor's wish list, or customer's uninformed opinion. Time spent chasing these sales is like burning your commission checks. You could have been investing your time pursuing real sales. The buyers at the top know where the money is and where it's going. Multiply the commission you received last year by 30% if you need to motivate yourself to use the ideas in this chapter.

2. STUDIES CONCLUDE THAT THE BEST SALESPEOPLE DO IT.

If you were the CEO of the largest computer company in world and your sales started dropping faster than you could say IBM, wouldn't you consider investigating what was happening with your sales force? When IBM commissioned a consulting firm to study their best salespeople (the ones whose sales were increasing in tough economic times), they discovered that calling on top executives was the skill that had the greatest impact on sales success. (*TABLE 13.1*) We've covered four of these skills already. It's time to tackle the one at the top of the list.

FIGURE 13.1: Sales Skills That Predict Success

1. Calling at the top

2. Consultative approach

3. Listening skills

4. Influencing skills

5. Questioning skills

3. THE COMPETITION IS NOWHERE IN SIGHT

The largest sale our Siemens division ever booked came from our connections at the top. As my manager and I started finalizing the details of the contract, the competitive sharks attacked from all angles. But they never penetrated this account where it counted most. They never met the senior Vice President of Finance, with whom we had earned an excellent business relationship. It took years to open that door, but once we were in, we noticed that the competition was nowhere to be seen. One of the reasons it's lonely at the top is that your competition isn't there.

4. YOU RECEIVE MORE ATTENTION AND BETTER TREATMENT WHEN CONNECTED AT THE TOP.

5. THE PARTNERSHIP YOU DEVELOP WITH YOUR CUSTOMER OVER THE LONG TERM WILL BE BASED ON BIGGER, BROADER ISSUES AND WILL LAST LONGER.

These last two benefits of calling at the top are from Barbara Geraghty's superb book, *Visionary Selling*.[2] If you are convinced you need to improve your skills in this area, follow the steps in this chapter *and* invest in her book. (www.visionaryselling.com)

Practical Techniques to Open Closed Doors

Before you can even think about entering the executive suite, you must to earn the right to knock on their door. And one of the best ways to earn this right is to develop a relationship with an inside coach, sometimes referred to as internal advocate.

You can find these coaches in a variety of places. In large accounts or complex sales, you might develop a coaching relationship with a mid-level manager with whom you had previous sales interactions. In strategic accounts, you could identify advocates during your S.T.A.T. session, as discussed in Chapter Ten. Having sales colleagues introduce you to people they know in an account or networking with top executives at association meetings are two other ways you might find these internal advocates.

Knowing somebody on the inside does not make him or her an inside advocate. If they are going to help you reach the top, they must satisfy four requirements:

→ Be sold on you and your product

→ Recognize how they benefit by helping you advance the sale

→ Obtain the information you need to prepare P.A.I.D. questions

→ Have influence with the top executives you need to reach

Once they are sold on you and your business solution, ask them to help you prepare for a meeting with the economic buyer. This can be tricky because coaches often act like gatekeepers for senior executives. To get them to open the gate for you, diplomatically ask critical questions they can't easily answer, but understand the need to address, such as:

1. What is your organization's strategic plan?

2. What are your organization's major goals for the next six months?

3. Where does the top executive feel most at risk?

4. Who does the top executive consider your biggest competitors?

5. What is keeping your top executives awake at night?

6. What assumptions should we make in our financial analysis?

7. How would you measure your success if you did invest in our services?

Most coaches understand why these questions are important, yet usually can't answer them. If the coach won't introduce you directly to the person you want, ask them to put you in touch with people who can provide the answers to these questions. Often the people who have the answers work with the executives.

For example, Don, a capital equipment salesman for Shimadzu, was trying to get an appointment with a Senior Vice President. But his internal coach, Mike, didn't think it was that important. During one phone conversation, Mike told Don that his Senior VP had requested that the finance department conduct a pro forma analysis of the purchase. (The pro forma is a "what if" analysis that allows one to assess the financial impact of a purchase depending on various scenarios and assumptions.) *Now's my chance,* Don thought. He proceeded to gently ask Mike several in-depth questions about the assumptions they would make in the analysis. Mike couldn't answer most of them. Don then asked Mike if he wanted to see how various assumptions affected the analysis, and thus the overall project. Mike jumped at the idea (probably because he would learn something new and be able to impress his Senior VP). Don also suggested that Mike invite the financial analyst (whom the Senior VP relied upon for these analyses). When the three of them met, Don shared his data and assumptions, many of which the analyst used in her pro forma. Although this financial analyst was not the economic buyer, she influenced him with her data.

Of course, the competition did muscle their way into the Senior VP's office near the end of the sale. But he took one look at their pro forma, told them he didn't agree with their assumptions, and informed them that the order was going to Don.

This story illustrates that the most effective method of reaching top executives is to develop a relationship with an internal advocate — someone who is willing to coach you through the sale. Yet that's not the only way to gain access to the top. Here are four other methods to get senior executives to open their closed doors:

1. CALL DURING OFF HOURS.

   Senior executives often get in early, stay late, and work on weekends. They have people screening the calls 8AM–5PM. Jodi, a former top saleswoman with Pfizer, told me that her customers often told her how impressed they were that she worked on Saturday mornings too.

2. WRITE A POWER LETTER.

In his audio program, *Selling To VITO,* (www.sellingtovito.com) Tony Parinello says that a captivating "power letter and envelope" should have the following characteristics:

LETTER

-→ Use plain white paper. No company stationery

-→ Write a headline across the top (like a newspaper) with a specific, bold benefit statement from a proof source. A quote usually works best.

-→ Compose a few specific benefits. Relate them to the recipient's strategic plan.

-→ End the letter by asking to meet to discuss how you might work together to get the same results your proof source in the headline received. Add a P.S. telling them when you will call their office to set up the meeting. *FIGURE 13.2* illustrates such a letter.

FIGURE 13.2: *Power Letters that Open Doors*

"Manna Supply Center increased sales 19% in the past six months. This is a direct result of the enhanced communication and information capability provided by the Strategy System we purchased from ABC Corp."

John Kensington
Director of Information Technology
Manna Supply Center

Ms. Executive
Chief Operating Officer
XYZ Supply Center

Dear Ms. Executive:

Manna Supply Center realized a $96,000 increase in revenue this year because of the successful implementation of our latest Strategy System. They have informed us that this added revenue will be used to purchase two new delivery trucks.

Additional benefits that Manna and other supply centers are experiencing as a result of a strategic business alliance with the ABC Corp. include the following:

#1 Improved customer satisfaction ratings
#2 More distribution contracts
#3 Increased order processing efficiency

We are helping many distribution centers achieve bottom-line results. We guarantee we can produce the same result for you.

Sincerely,
John B. Goode
ABC, Corp.
(310) 123-4567

P.S. I will call your office November 21 at 8:30 a.m. to schedule a brief meeting. If you will not be in, please leave word with your assistant Erin as to the best time to call you back. Thank you.

Letters like these increase the chances that you will get a response. It shows you know their business, understand their pain, and can discuss possible prescriptions. Change the words to reflect your style and business solutions, and then see how it works for you.

ENVELOPE

→ Mail in a large white envelope (9 x 12)

→ Handwrite the address, no return labels or company logos

→ Use your name (not the company's)

→ Apply regular stamps

3. BRING IN THE BOSS.

Arrange a meeting that includes your manager. This is another way to get your foot in the executive's door. Professional courtesy often obligates an executive to meet when someone of a similar title calls (i.e., your boss's office). The risk in taking this step is that your customer may want a relationship with your boss, not you. Here are a few tips to help you stay in control when you bring in your big guns to meet the customer's top gun:

→ Ask your manager's secretary to set up the meeting for you. Make sure he or she refers to it as *your* meeting, not your boss's.

→ Prepare your executive for the call. What should be said, asked, and negotiated?

→ Discuss how your executive intends to send the clear message that *you* have the responsibility and authority for this account. Suggest that your boss adhere to the following guidelines:

  a. Allow you to start and facilitate the meeting

  b. Defer to you throughout the meeting

  c. Ask you to explore areas of potential collaboration during the meeting

   d. Let you summarize the meeting's action steps

   e. End the meeting by telling your customer how you will
      follow up with them

4. GO OUT ON A LIMB.

In *Visionary Selling,* Barbara Geraghty reminds us that the folks at
the "C" level (CEO, CFO, CIO...) love to be challenged. The same
old song and dance bores them. She recommends that you identify
an element of your solution that is controversial or provocative.

What to Say When You're Face to Face With the Top Gun

The call to the top follows the fundamentals outlined throughout this
book. Since repetition is the mother of skill, let's review the keys to the
science and soul of an effective sales call.

PREPARE FOR THE CALL

Plan to shine as the business expert. Even if you bring in your boss, your
customer must see that you are the one leading the effort to solve their
problems, based on your deep knowledge about their business. I have
been in many meetings where the primary salesperson disappeared in
the shadow of a brilliant sales team. Make sure you plan how you will
conduct the meeting and show your knowledge of their business.

Discuss their business issues with your inside advocate. Use their
insight to create the P.A.I.D. questions to ask during the executive meeting.
Your questions must address their strategic issues. Strategy is what
commands an executive's attention. It should dominate your preparation.

OPEN THE CALL

Executives are too busy for idle chatter. They know why you're there.
After the introductions, take control of the meeting by addressing the
purpose of the meeting, followed by a Present circumstance question.
For example:

You: (not your boss) "Ms. Executive, thanks for taking the time to meet with us today. The reason we wanted to talk with you was to discuss how we might be able to work together to decrease your inventory costs. In meeting with some of your people during the past few weeks, they indicated that you wanted to cut these costs by 30% during the next year. Is this your top priority?"

Ms. Executive: "Yes, cutting inventory costs is my top priority."

You: (Present circumstance) "Are you still looking for suppliers to work with you on a new inventory system customized for your environment?"

Ms. Executive: "No, not really. We hired a few sharp programmers who know how to modify the software, once we get an off-the-shelf package. We're looking for a company to give us a great price and fast delivery. You can do that, right?"

CONDUCT THE CALL

Now, conduct the call using the P.A.I.D. approach. For example:

You: (Present circumstance) "Of course, great pricing is part of our package. And before we get to that, may I ask you a quick question about modifying the software?"

Ms. Executive: "Sure."

You: (Present circumstance) "When you say you hired good people to modify the software you intend to purchase, would they be part of Davey Jones's new programming team?"

Ms. Executive: "Why, yes. How do you know him?"

You: (you have done your homework) "I spoke with him last week to make sure we could meet your delivery requirements. One of the issues that he brought up was the need to have bar code input."

Ms. Executive: (practically interrupting you) "Oh yes, he wants all the bells and whistles. I've told him several times we just can't afford it this year. Now, getting back to pricing, what can you do for us?"

You: (Present circumstance) "I think you'll be very pleased with our pricing, based on my discussions with Mack, your material management manager. One last thing before we get to price; you track your inventory using the desk-top entry approach, correct?"

Ms. Executive: "Yes."

You: (Area of concern question) "What problems does that create with tracking the flow of your supplies that arrive at different docks?"

Ms. Executive: "At times we have had a hard time tracking inventory."

You: (Impact question) "How has that affected your production lines?"

Ms. Executive: "We're having discussions about how to keep those lines moving."

You: (Impact question) "Have you calculated the cost of shutting down one line for a day due to inventory shortages?"

Ms. Executive: "Yes. That's why it's a problem. It costs us about $100,000.00 when a line goes down."

Your Boss: (Impact question) "And if a new inventory system comes on line, leaving you with even less inventory on hand, how will that impact the problem?"

Ms. Executive: "We haven't discussed that yet, but we'll have to come up with something."

You: (summarizing and Impact question) "Ms. Executive, let me see if I understand this: You have an inventory flow issue that costs about $100,000.00 every time you shut down. And this might become an even bigger problem when you decrease your inventory?"

Ms. Executive: "Yeah, don't remind me."

You: (Area of concern question) "Last question: Have you determined what the additional personnel costs would be if you increase the traffic due to lower inventory?"

Ms. Executive: "Yes, we know we would have to add one more person at about $50,000.00. But that would be more than compensated for by the lower inventory costs."

You: (Determine benefit question) "Ms. Executive, if you could avoid the expense of hiring a new person, and keep your production line moving, what would you guess you could save per year?"

Ms. Executive: "Well, *if* that were possible, I guess I would have to say about $240,000, based on being down two full days last year."

Your Boss: (prescribing and earning agreement) "Ms. Executive, would it be helpful if your staff and our team put together a draft pro forma for a new just-in-time inventory system? We've done this for other companies, as you can see in this document. I think we could show you how to decrease your inventory costs by both lowering your personnel costs and eliminating the production downtime. We should be able to save you at least $240,000.00 in the first year."

Ms. Executive: "That sounds very interesting. Maybe you, Mr. Jones, and one of my finance people should put something together."

You: "Great, I'll set it up. And then get back to you, OK?"

This scenario illustrates why executives agree to take the next step with salespeople who use science and soul to reach their goal. The science on this call included having a pre-call objective (that this customer would agree to a pro forma analysis), playing two roles (applying consulting and team leadership), and asking P.A.I.D. questions during the call. The soulful approach to selling was illustrated by *Being Real* (no phony chitchat), *Being Present* (no distractions), and *Being Deep* (knowing their business issues). When you remember to use science and soul when you call on top executives, you'll open closed doors and increase your long-term sales success.

The Paradox of Selling

To fully integrate the teachings of science and the soul, and express the paradox between these two in selling, we conclude our journey together by transforming the S3 Equation (*FIGURE 13.1*) into a new S3 Model. (*FIGURE 13.2*). In the new model, the scientific tactics influencing each of the three major variables during a sales call are positioned in the outer ring. This is because customers are in the external environment, outside the circle, and your contact with them occurs via the sales call. The scientific strategies affecting long-term sales success are in the middle ring because they are removed from your day-to-day customer interaction, but directly affect your sales over the long haul. And the soul principles are now positioned in the center, because they represent the heart of the model and the core of who you are.

The circular shape of the S3 Model illustrates the interdependence of science and soul on your journey of sales success. Growing your COMMITMENT, BELIEF, and FEEDBACK over time requires applying all of these tools. If you underuse any of the short-term tactics or long-term strategies, your circle loses its shape (i.e., you get a flat) and your sales will probably stall. On the other hand, if you overuse any of these tools while neglecting the others, you could become strong to a fault (i.e., you get a bubble). This overuse creates a bumpy ride, and eventually your bubble will burst.

The new S3 Model also illustrates the tension you may feel as you apply the scientific tactic and strategies (outer and middle rings), while growing the soul principles (inner ring). For example, as you increase your commitment to reach your sales goals using science (by focusing on *Value* or playing the *Role* customers want you to play), you may find it a stretch to be you (the soul principle of *Be Real*). Similarly, as you strengthen your belief that you will achieve your goals (by *Modeling* sales skills or practicing the art of *Mastery*), you might feel stressed trying to *Be Present* with your customer at the same time. Finally, you could feel the tension between the feedback of selling (using daily rewards as *Motivation* or your company's commission *System*) and the desire to serve your customers better (the soul principle of *Be Deep*).

These are all examples of the paradoxical nature of selling today. The older I get the grayer and more paradoxical things seem. Life is not as black and white as it once was. We are living in a smaller, more interdependent world. We need new approaches to help us see these connections, understand their ramifications, and manage the tensions. Keep the new S3 Model in front of you as a reminder to embrace the paradox and interdependence of sales. Look at the model as you sell your way through the day. How surprised will you be when your sales really blast off? The model predicts this increase because the science of the selling helps you improve the sales process, while the soul of selling reminds you to improve the salesperson.

FIGURE 13.1: The Selling with Science & Soul Equation™

SALES GOAL =	COMMITMENT	BELIEF	FEEDBACK
Sales-call tactic	*Value*	*Modeling*	*Motivation*
Selling strategy	*Role*	*Mastery*	*Systems*
Soul principle	*Real*	*Present*	*Deep*

FIGURE 13.2: *The Selling with Science & Soul Model*™

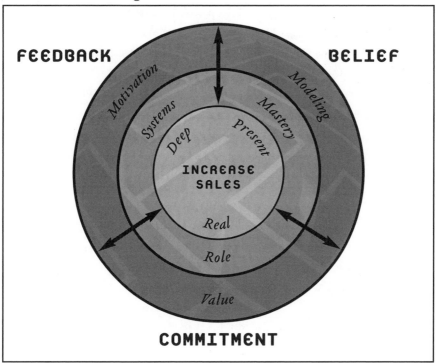

Sales is a Wonderful Life

The opening chapter told the story about all the salespeople who gave me three more years with my father, years when words unspoken were finally spoken. I'll always be thankful for the extra time Dad and I had together. And as you and I end our time together (but continue our adventure *through* each other), I'd like to share a closing sales story that my father told me during those last few years.

One day, my Dad invited a salesperson to our home to show us a contraption designed to address my childhood bed-wetting. (Though they never made a big deal out of it, my parents and I were tired of this problem.) The "bed-wetting machine" was a screen mesh (placed under the sheet), hooked up to a huge, car-size battery. If I started to wet the bed, a screeching alarm would go off. The whole thing scared the crap out of me. Dad bought it anyway.

As my father walked the salesman out our front door to the car, Dad saw me throwing acorns in the shadow of our giant oak tree. He yelled at me to stop, which I did. The salesperson reached for his car door, turned to my Dad and said something that I couldn't hear, but changed my life (and maybe yours).

A few years before he died, my father told me that the salesman had said something like, "Mr. Jensen, you have a fine family. Your second son, Dave, has a wonderful independent and confident streak in him. Please don't crush it." Dad stood on the side of the road and watched the salesman drive down our hill. I picked up another acorn.

My father told me that from that day on, he always tried to celebrate, not crush, my independent and confident inner spirit. He said an acorn turns into an oak tree because that's what's inside. In the last few years we had together, Dad reminded me of this incident because he believed the bed-wetting-machine salesman had much to do with who I had become. Dad believed the salesperson not only sold a machine that made a difference to our family, but that his words had a lasting influence on many lives. Today, I'm convinced Dad was right. (Oh yeah, in case you're wondering, the bed-wetting machine worked!)

Speaking of today, it is Christmas morning! The sun is up, kids are playing in the street with their new toys, and the movie, *It's A Wonderful Life*, is on television again. To me, the spirit of the bed-wetting story and this movie are the same: *Your sales and your life make a difference to more people than you probably realize.*

We started this book by saying that sales can be divided into two parts, the sales process and the salesperson. My hope is that this book helps you improve your processes of selling, because, like the salesman in my bed-wetting story and George (the main character in the movie who is a banker and a great salesman), your sales make a big difference to your customers and their families. I also hope this book helps *you* grow, because, like the bed-wetting-machine salesman and George, who you are makes a BIG difference to many people every day. THAT's why it's a wonderful life. My prayer is that *Selling with Science and Soul*™ makes life even more wonderful for you and all those you touch every day.

Thank you.

APPENDIX A

Acknowledgments

This book could not have been written if weren't for the incredible support from my teachers, collaborators, friends and family, and students.

To the many teachers who have shown me how to use the tools of science to pursue the truth, I say thank you. Special appreciation goes to Dr. Victor Froelicher who believed in what I could do, Dr. Eddie Atwood who believed in me, and Dr. Mike Sullivan who reminded me about the limits of science. These wonderful teachers became great friends and kept my candle burning during the early years. More recently, Ahmed and Laurie Yehia and Dr. Peter Koestenbaum have shown me how to apply the philosophy of leadership in selling and in all I do.

If this book integrates science and soul well, it is because several friends and colleagues contributed their practical sales experience and life-long wisdom. Ken Dorio, Jim Montgomery, Brian Dehm, Jodi Walker, Jon Williams, Tom Owens, and Jay Ashworth deserve a warm embrace. They helped transform my rambling ideas about selling into an organized book. In addition, my dear friend and professional storyteller Karen Golden counseled me to seed this book with the transforming energy of stories. And of course, I thank my editor Penny Post, who slashed my last draft to bits, demonstrating how much I still need to grow as a writer. I am deeply in debt to all these terrific collaborators.

Writing this book as I was growing my speaking and consulting business was really hard. It's difficult to find the words to thank my family and friends for their encouraging words and affirming spirit during this arduous adventure. It's even harder to express my gratitude for a lifetime of love, support, and inspiration they have given me. But here it goes:

Bob Gunning and Bill Skinner were my very first mentors. They also became great friends who gave me the confidence to believe in my dreams. John and Lee Sirotnak reminded to look for my answers in the dancing flames of the campfire. My rock-n-roll buddy Mike Amato inspired me to follow the hero's journey. He heard the call, moved west, descended into the abyss, overcame the challenges, and brought music to the world. Kris Nebel showed me the power of faith and taught me that life is mostly about the little things every day. MaryRose Patejak patiently listened to my woes and encouraged me every step of the way. Susan Goulet prayed for me and stayed with me during my dark night of the soul. My brothers and sister (and their terrific children), as well as Aunt Viv and Uncle Joe, always welcomed me home with open arms and machinegun wisecracks. They, along with Mom and Dad's legacy, provided the fertile soil for me to grow. And to my angel Irene, who is the spark in my heart. She helps me shine my light by shinning her's.

Finally, I am infinitely grateful to the thousands of participants who have attended my workshops and seminars over the years. Indirectly, and sometimes very directly, they continually challenged me to teach the science with my soul. I've become much more real, present and deep because of them. These wonderful students were my teachers whose critical feedback now fills these pages.

I close by thanking the good Lord for working through me as I wrote the book. I tried to listen to His word as I composed the ones you've read.

APPENDIX B

Quotations to Sell By

I've done the best I can to ensure that the quotations throughout the book are accurate in both content and attribution. The quotations without a name ascribed to them are, to the best of my knowledge, "mine." I put mine in quotes because I've been influenced by so many wonderful people (through their books, seminars, audio programs, and friendships) that I don't feel the quotations are completely mine. So feel free to use them in any way you deem appropriate.

Here are a few more (with proper attribution) that might help you sell with more science and soul.

GOALS

"The 'what' must come before the 'how.'"

 —JULIA CAMERON

"You are not responsible for the thoughts that come to mind, only those invited to stay."

 —LIN MOREL

"There are in fact two things, science and opinion; the former begets knowledge, the later ignorance."

 —HIPPOCRATES

"Any business that doesn't bring in new business will soon be out of business."
—JOE GENNARO

COMMITMENT

"You can get anything in life you want if you help enough people get what they want."
—ZIG ZIGLAR

"You have teamwork if you see an abundance of frankness, humor, wit, and simplicity."
—THOMAS MOORE

REAL

"While an original is always hard to find, it's always easy to recognize."
—JOHN MASON

"Giving a facelift to a corpse does not give it life."
—BISHOP JOHN SHELBY SPONG

"If you are just then your works are also just."
—MATHEW FOX

"If you want to work on your art, work on your life."
—CHEKHOV

"Do not mistake personality for character."
—WILMA ASKINAS

"May the outward and inward man be one."
—SOCRATES

"We must be the change we wish to see in the world."
—MAHATMA GANDHI

BELIEF

"We don't get what we pray for, we get what we believe."
—REV. MICHAEL BECKWITH

*"Whatever you ask for in prayer,
believe you have received it, and it will be yours."*
—MARK 11:24

"Beliefs are rules for action."
—WILLIAM JAMES

*"Nothing is easier than self-deceit; for what each of us wishes,
we also believe to be true."*
—DEMOSTHENES

*"I have said, you are gods; all of you are children
of the most high…"*
—PSALM 82:6

"We become what we think about."
—EARL NIGHTENGALE

PRESENT

"Millions long for immortality, but don't know what to do on a rainy day."
—SUSAN ERTZ

"Think about things that are pure and lovely, and dwell on the fine, good things in others."
—PHILIPPIANS 4:8B

"He who cannot do what he wants, let him want what he can do."
—LEONARD DA VINCI

"Framed in space beauty blooms."
—ANNE LYNBERG

"Keep your eyes on the road and your hands upon the wheel."
—JIM MORRISON

"It's how we go through our day that brings our soul to the surface."
—SAM KEEN

"That which has come to pass, has come to pass. So, let it pass."
—REV. MICHAEL BECKWITH

"What does the barber say? Next!"
—JIM MONTGOMERY

FEEDBACK

"You must learn from the mistakes of others.
You can't possibly live long enough to make them all yourself."
—SAM LEVENSON

"All man's miseries derive from
not being able to sit quietly in a room alone."
—PASCAL

"All life is an experiment.
The more experiments you make, the better."
—RALPH WALDO EMERSON

"Do not confuse tunnel vision for focus."
—AHMED YEHIA

DEEP

"Soul is not a thing, but a quality or a dimension
of experiencing life and ourselves."
—THOMAS MOORE

"*Knowing your own darkness is the best method for dealing with the darkness in other people.*"
—CARL JUNG

"*The monk in hiding himself from the world becomes not less a person, but more of a person, more truly and perfectly himself.*"
—THOMAS MERTON

"*We are meaning making machines.*"
—REV. MICHAEL BECKWITH

APPENDIX C

The Selling with Science & Soul Quiz

If you are picking this book up for the first time you might be asking questions like: Can this book really increase my sales? Will it be worth my time and money? Is there anything truly new in selling? As the biased author, I can't answer these questions for you. But you can answer them yourself by taking a short quiz. The first two statements are fill-in-the-blank, the rest are True-False. The answers are in the next section.

1. The #1 key to persuasiveness is _____ .
2. The belief that best predicts sales success is _____ .
3. As objections increase, sales-call success decreases.
4. Customers devalue what they currently own before they buy something new.
5. Executives rank a personal relationship with a salesperson as important.
6. Customers want salespeople to be consultants.
7. Having difficult goals or quotas increases sales.
8. Listening to subliminal audio-programs increases sales success.
9. Regularly reminding salespeople about their quotas increase sales success.
10. These questions help you see the value of adding science and soul to your selling. (True or False bonus question)

The Selling with Science & Soul Answers

1. Expertise   (CHAPTER 3, Section: *Be Deep*)
2. Self-efficacy   (CHAPTER 6, Section: *Take a Hike*)
3. True   (CHAPTER 7, Section: *Just Say "Know" to Objections*)
4. True   (CHAPTER 7, Section: *How Customers Really Buy*)
5. False   (CHAPTER 10, Section: *Is Relationship Selling Dead?*)
6. False   (CHAPTER 9, Section: *Why You Are Not a Consultant*)
7. True   (CHAPTER 4, Section: *Get S.M.A.R.T.–*
                      Research from 393 Goal Studies)
8. False   (CHAPTER 6, Section: *R. U. Driving to Sales Success?*)
9. False   (CHAPTER 6, Section: Self-efficacy –
                      The Science of Believing)
10. True   (THE WHOLE BOOK: *Selling with Science & Soul*)

So how did you do? If you got them all right, close the book, give me a call, and let's get you teaching this stuff. If you answered more than half correctly, you get a gold star. If you missed more than half don't feel too badly, you have a lot of company. Most salespeople miss at least 50%, not because they don't know how to sell, but because they never learned how to use science and soul to increase sales…UNTIL NOW! So, what are you waiting for? Dive into this book and watch your sales take off.

APPENDIX D

References

CHAPTER 1: *How To Use Science To Increase Sales*

1. *USA Today,* February 9: 2A, 1999.

2. Steveson H and Moldoveanu CM: THE POWER OF PREDICTABILITY. *Harvard Business Review,* July–August: 140–142, 1995.

CHAPTER 2: *Why You Need More Soul In Your Selling*

1. Ferguson T and Lee J: SPIRITUAL REALITY. *Forbes,* January 27: 70–76, 1997.

2. CAREERS: THE SOUL AT WORK. *The Los Angeles Times,* April 6: 1–60, 1998.

3. SPIRITUALITY IS THE LATEST BUZZWORD. *U.S. News & World Report,* May 3: 46, 1999.

4. Tischler L: CAN KEVIN ROLLINS FIND THE SOUL OF DELL, *Fast Company,* November: 110–114, 2002.

5. Friedman R: THE CASE OF THE RELIGIOUS NETWORK GROUP. *Harvard Business Review,* July–August: 28–38, 1999.

6. Rause V: THE SCIENCE OF GOD: SEARCHING FOR THE DIVINE. *Readers Digest,* December: 140–145, 2001.

7. Gunther M: GOD AND BUSINESS. *Fortune,* July 9: 58–80, 2001.

8. Ferguson T and Lee J: COIN OF THE NEW AGE. *Forbes,* September 9: 86, 1996.

9. Miles J: PRIME TIME'S SEARCH FOR GOD. *TV Guide,* March 29: 24, 1997.

10. Clayton P: THE ULTIMATE HYPOTHESIS. *Forbes ASAP,* October 4: 241–242, 1999.

11. Shermer M: *How We Believe: The Search for God in an Age of Science.* W.H. Freeman and Company, New York: 2000.

12. Roof W: *Spiritual Marketplace: Baby Boomers and the Remaking of American Religion.* Princeton University Press, Princeton: 1999.

13. Gunther M: GOD AND BUSINESS. *Fortune,* July 9: 64, 2001.

14. Ziglar Z: *The Autobiography of Zig Ziglar.* Random House, New York: 108, 2002.

CHAPTER 3: *How To Add More Soul In Your Selling*

1. McKenna R: MARKETING IS EVERYTHING. *Harvard Business Review,* 69: 65–79, 1991.

2. Cameron J and Bryan M: *The Artist Way.* G.P. Putnam's Sons: New York, 1992.

3. Robbins A: *Unlimited Power.* Fawcett Columbine Book: New York, 1986.

4. Moore T: *Care of the Soul.* HarperCollins: New York, 1992.

5. Hilman J: *Blue Flame.* HarperCollins: New York, 1989, 54.

6. Seligman M: *Learned Optimism.* Simon & Schuster: New York, 1990.

7. Fiske S: FORECASTING THE FUTURE. *Psychology Today.* November/December: 33, 2002.

8. Rosenthal R and Rubin D: INTERPERSONAL EXPECTANCY EFFECTS: THE FIRST 345 STUDIES. *The Behavioral and Brain Sciences* 3: 377–415, 1978.

9. Wilson E and Sherrell D: SOURCE EFFECTS IN COMMUNICATION AND PERSUASION RESEARCH: A META-ANALYSIS OF EFFECT SIZE. *Journal of the Academy of Marketing Science* 21(2): 101–112, 1993.

10. Campbell J: *Creative Mythology: The Masks of God.* Penguin Group: New York, 574, 1968.

11. Shermer M: *How We Believe: The Search for God in an Age of Science.* W. H. Freeman and Company: New York, 127, 2000.

CHAPTER 4: *Knowing Where You're Going*

1. Locke E and Latham G: *A Theory of Goal Setting & Task Performance.* Prentice Hall: Englewood Cliffs, 1990.

2. Barrick M, Mount M, Strauss J, et al: CONSCIENTIOUS AND PERFORMANCE OF SALES REPRESENTATIVES: TEST OF THE MEDIATING EFFECTS OF GOAL SETTING. *Journal of Applied Psychology* 78(5): 715–722, 1993.

3. Hollenbeck J and Williams C: GOAL IMPORTANCE, SELF-FOCUS, AND THE GOAL-SETTING PROCESS. *Journal of Applied Psychology* 72(2): 204–211, 1987.

4. Senge P: *The Fifth Discipline: The Art and Practice of the Learning Organization.* Doubleday: New York, 1990.

5. Chowdhury J: THE MOTIVATIONAL IMPACT OF SALES QUOTAS ON SALES EFFORT. *Journal of Marketing Research* 30: 28–41, 1993.

6. IBID. 1, p307.

7. Ziglar Z: *Over The Top.* Thomas Nelson: Nashville, 105, 1994.

8. Goldman B, Masterson S, Locke E, Groth, M, Jensen D: GOAL-DIRECTEDNESS AND PERSONAL IDENTITY AS CORRELATES OF LIFE OUTCOMES. *Psychological Reports* 91: 153–166, 2002.

CHAPTER 5: *Should You Be Committed?*

1. Locke E and Latham G: *A Theory of Goal Setting & Task Performance.* Prentice Hall, Englewood Cliffs: 151, 1990.

2. Kanter R: COLLABORATIVE ADVANTAGE: THE ART OF ALLIANCES. *Harvard Business Review,* July–August: 96–108, 1994.

CHAPTER 6: *How Do You Spell Belief?*

1. Berry J and West R: COGNITIVE SELF-EFFICACY IN RELATION TO PERSONAL MASTERY AND GOAL SETTING ACROSS THE LIFE SPAN. *International Journal of Behavioral Development* 16(2): 351–379, 1993.

2. Sujan H, Weitz B, Kumar N, et al: LEARNING ORIENTATION, WORKING SMART AND EFFECTIVE SELLING. *Journal of Marketing* 58: 39–52, 1994.

3. Barling J and Beattie R: SELF-EFFICACY AND SALES PERFORMANCE. *Journal of Organizational Behavior Management* 5: 41–51, 1983.

4. Gist M and Mitchell T: SELF-EFFICACY: A THEORETICAL ANALYSIS OF ITS DETERMINANTS AND MALLEABILITY. *Academy of Management Review* 17(2): 183–211, 1992.

5. Brooks V: *The Life of Emerson.* E.P. Dutton & Co: New York, 270, 1932.

6. Hill N: *Think and Grow Rich.* Fawcett Crest Book: New York, 1937.

7. Gardner H: *Creating Minds.* HarperCollins: New York, 385, 1993.

8. Greenwald A, Spangenberg E, Pratkanis A, et al: DOUBLE-BLIND TESTS OF SUBLIMINAL SELF-HELP AUDIO-TAPES. *Psychological Science* 2 (2): 119–122, 1991.

9. I WILL LOVE THIS STORY. *U.S. News & World Report.* May, 12: 12, 1997.

10. Watson D and Thorpe R: *Self-Directed Behavior: Self-Modification for Personal Adjustment.* Brooks/Cole Publishing Company: Pacific Grove, 57, 1989.

CHAPTER 7: *Modeling 37,750 Sales Calls*

1. Woodruff R, Schumann D, Gardial S, et al: UNDERSTANDING VALUE AND SATISFACTION FROM THE CUSTOMER'S POINT OF VIEW. *Survey of Business* 29 (1): 33–40, 1993.

2. Bunn M: TAXONOMY OF BUYING DECISION APPROACHES. *Journal of Marketing* 57 (1): 38–56, 1993.

3. Bless H, Mackie D, and Schwarz N: MOOD EFFECT ON ATTITUDE JUDGMENTS: INDEPENDENT EFFECTS OF MOOD BEFORE AND AFTER MESSAGE ELABORATION. *Journal of Personality and Social Psychology* 63 (4): 585–595, 1992.

4. Ambady N and Rosenthal R: THIN SLICES OF EXPRESSIVE BEHAVIOR AS PREDICTORS OF INTERPERSONAL CONSEQUENCES: A META-ANALYSIS. *Psychological Bulletin* 111(2): 256–274, 1992.

5. Rackham N: *SPIN Selling*. McGraw-Hill: New York, 1988.

6. Rackham N: WHY CLOSING IS BAD FOR SALES. *Marketing,* April 16: 65–66, 1980.

7. IBID. 5.

8. Peck S: *The Road Less Traveled*. Touchstone: New York, 1978.

CHAPTER 8: *Using Feedback Stay To Motivated All Day*

1. Locke E and Latham G: *A Theory of Goal Setting & Task Performance*. Prentice Hall: Englewood Cliffs, 192, 1990.

2. Kim J: EFFECT OF BEHAVIOR PLUS OUTCOME GOAL SETTING AND FEEDBACK ON EMPLOYEE SATISFACTION AND PERFORMANCE. *Academy of Management Journal* 27(1): 139–149, 1984.

3. Dubinsky A, Yammarino F, Jolson M, et al: CLOSENESS OF SUPERVISION AND SALESPERSON WORK OUTCOMES: AN ALTERNATIVE PERSPECTIVE. *Journal of Business Research* 29: 225–237, 1994.

4. DelVecchio S: PREDICTING SALES MANAGER CONTROL: A COMPARISON OF CONTROL SYSTEMS AND LEADERSHIP APPROACHES. *Journal of Applied Business Research* 12 (4): 100–114, 1996.

5. Brande D: *Wake Up and Live*. Cornerstone Library: New York, 1936.

6. Darwin C: *The Expression of Emotion in Man and Animals*. University of Chicago Press: Chicago, 1965. (Original manuscript published in 1872.)

7. James W: *Principles of Psychology* (Vol. 2). Dover: New York, 1950. (Original manuscript published in 1890.)

8. Izard C: FOUR SYSTEMS FOR EMOTION ACTIVATION: COGNITIVE AND NON-COGNITIVE PROCESS. *Psychological Review* 100: 68–90, 1993.

9. deMello A: *Awareness: The Perils and Opportunities or Reality.* Doubleday: New York, 1990, 28.

CHAPTER 9: *How To Add Consulting To Your Selling*

1. Churchill G, Ford N, Harley, S et al: THE DETERMINANTS OF SALESPERSON PERFORMANCE: A META-ANALYSIS. *Journal of Marketing Research* 22: 103–118, 1985.

2. Johnston M, Parasuraman A, Futrell C, Black, W: A LONGITUDINAL ASSESSMENT OF THE IMPACT OF SELECTED ORGANIZATIONAL INFLUENCES ON SALESPEOPLE'S ORGANIZATIONAL COMMITMENT DURING EARLY EMPLOYMENT. *Journal of Marketing Research* 27: 333–344, 1990.

3. Michaels R, Cron W, Dubinsky A: INFLUENCE ON THE ORGANIZATIONAL COMMITMENT AND WORK ALIENATION OF SALESPEOPLE AND INDUSTRIAL BUYERS. *Journal of Marketing Research* 25: 363–383, 1988.

4. Lippitt G and Lippitt R: *The Consulting Process In Action.* University Associates: San Diego, 1986.

5. Wilson E and Sherrell D: SOURCE EFFECTS IN COMMUNICATION AND PERSUASION RESEARCH: A META-ANALYSIS OF EFFECT SIZE. *Journal of the Academy of Marketing Science* 21(2): 101–112, 1993.

6. *Reinventing the Sales Organization.* The Conference Board: New York, Report Number 1102–95–CH. 1995.

7. Drucker, P: *Management Tasks, Responsibilities, Practices.* Harper & Row: New York, 64, 1973.

8. Miller R and Heiman S: *Strategic Selling.* Warner Books: New York, 1985.

9. Johnson L: THE REAL VALUE OF CUSTOMER LOYALTY. *MIT Sloan Management Review* Winter: 14–17, 2002.

CHAPTER 10: *How To Add Teamwork To Your Selling*

1. Chase L: DETERMINANTS OF SELLING EFFECTIVENESS: DELIVERING VALUE-ADDED: IS YOUR SALES FORCE MEETING THE CUSTOMER'S EXPECTATIONS? *American Salesman* 40 (2): 11–15, 1995.

2. Trent R, Monczka R, and Kaeufer K: EFFECTIVE CROSS-FUNCTIONAL SOURCING TEAMS: CRITICAL SUCCESS FACTORS. *International Journal of Purchasing and Materials Management* 30 (4): 3–11, 1994.

3. Ancona D, Bresman H, and Kaeufer K: THE COMPARATIVE ADVANTAGE OF X-TEAMS. *MIT Sloan Management Review* Spring: 33–39, 2002.

4. Koestenbaum, P: *Leadership: The Inner Side of Greatness.* Jossey-Bass: San Francisco, 2002.

5. IBID 4, p10.

CHAPTER 11: *Mastery Says, Sweat The Small Stuff*

1. Berry J and West R: COGNITIVE SELF-EFFICACY IN RELATION TO PERSONAL MASTERY AND GOAL SETTING ACROSS THE LIFE SPAN. *International Journal of Behavioral Development* 16(2): 351–379, 1993.

2. Sexton T, Tuckman B, Crehan K, et al: AN INVESTIGATION OF THE PATTERNS OF SELF-EFFICACY, OUTCOME EXPECTATION, OUTCOME VALUE, AND PERFORMANCE ACROSS TRIALS. *Cognitive Therapy and Research* 16(3): 329–348, 1992.

3. Bloom B: *Developing Talent in Young People.* Random House: New York, 1985.

4. Covey S: *The 7 Habits of Highly Effective People.* Simon and Schuster: 47, 1989.

CHAPTER 12: *Systems Of Feedback Keep You On Track*

1. Merton T: *The Seven Storey Mountain.* Harcourt Brace Jovanovich: New York, 82, 1948.

2. Hilman J: *Blue Flame.* HarperCollins: New York, 54 1989.

3. Dyer W: *Wisdom of the Ages.* HarperCollins: New York, 242, 1998.

4. Moore T: *Care of the Soul.* HarperCollins: New York, 47, 1992.

5. Miller, J: *QBQ: The Question Behind the Question.* Denver Press: Denver, 2001.

CHAPTER 13: *How To Sell To Top Executives*

1. Peoples D. *Selling to the Top.* John Wiley & Sons: New York, 1993.

2. Geraghty B. *Visionary Selling.* Simon & Schuster: New York, 1998.